WRIGHT-SIZED HOUSES

FRANK LLOYD WRIGHT'S SOLUTIONS FOR MAKING SMALL HOUSES FEEL BIG

DIANE MADDEX

ABRAMS · NEW YORK

CONTENTS

INTRODUCTION

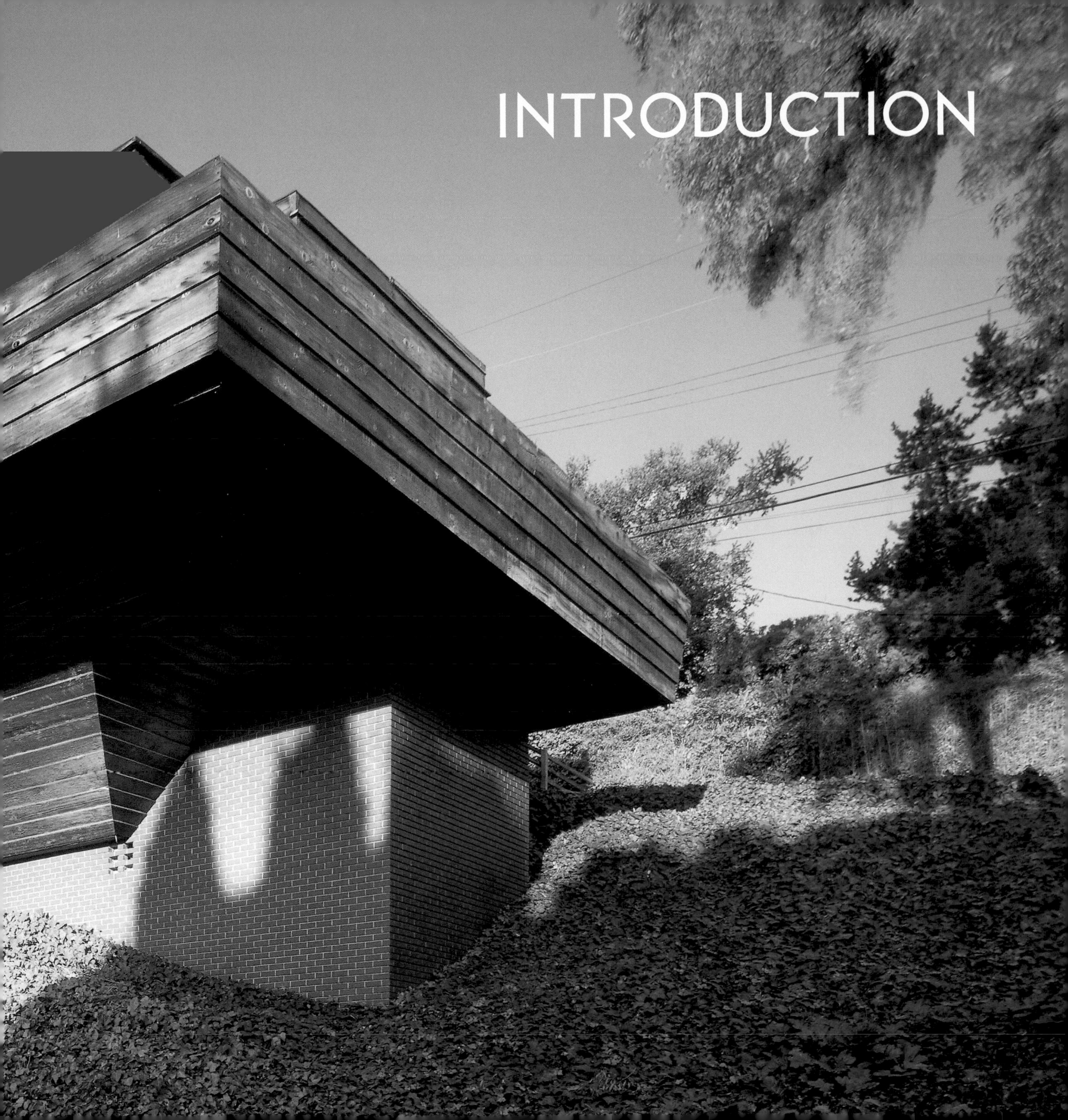

When Wright designed his first house, his own home (1889) in Oak Park, Illinois, he included space for a studio on the second floor so he could moonlight in the evenings (opposite). After his children were born, he used a partial wall to divide the space into girls' and boys' bedrooms. In the 1950s, by then in his eighties, he was still wrestling with how best to design small houses in places such as Usonia Homes in Pleasantville, New York (above).

Frank Lloyd Wright (1867–1959) is remembered around the world as the architect of Fallingwater, the Robie House, and the Guggenheim Museum. His greatest legacy, however, involves something far more modest: small houses built for average families. Wright was above all an architect of houses, and it was the small house that challenged him his entire career. "The house of moderate cost is not only America's major architectural problem but the problem most difficult for her major architects," he admitted in 1954, referring of course to himself. Six decades after he began trying to solve the small-house problem, it remained a challenge—as it still is today.

Yet Wright succeeded in showing that even cottages could be designed with dignity and integrity. We can see the imprint of his genius in architectural features that many of us take for granted: walls of windows to capture vistas, exterior materials repeated inside, great rooms inspired by his open plans, dining alcoves tucked into the main living area, bedrooms in quiet zones, decks that extend interiors into outdoor rooms, a carport to house the family car. His ideas were revolutionary a century ago, but the inescapable fact is that the revolution has not been won. Many of Wright's sensible housing solutions have been overlooked in the rush to turn homes into opulent showcases that tend to look backward rather than forward.

At the beginning of the twenty-first century, the average size of new single-family American houses had crept up to about 2,300 square feet, and they cost more than $200,000 despite the decline in family size. In 1900, when Wright was in the first years of his seven-decade career, a typical home was just 700

Wright lost no time in lecturing and writing about his new architectural ideas, beginning just a year after he opened his own practice in 1893. By 1901 popular magazines such as the *Ladies' Home Journal* were eager to showcase his innovations. One plan published by the magazine in 1907, for a "Fireproof House for $5,000," was adapted the next year for Wright's Stockman House in Mason City, Iowa (above). He moved the entrance and stairs to the side so he could open up the plan of the house's first floor.

to 1,200 square feet and cost less than $5,000, a considerable outlay even so for a typical family earning about $490 a year. Now many people, seeking to reverse this explosion in size, are looking for not-so-big houses that reflect the harmony and simplicity that Wright built into his residential designs.

Other innovators such as Orson Squire Fowler, with his octagonal houses in the nineteenth century; Le Corbusier, with his twentieth-century machines for living; and Buckminster Fuller, with his shiny round Dymaxion House, have all tackled the question of what a middle-class home should look like. But none has had a lasting effect to compare with Wright's. This preacher's son from Wisconsin somehow delved deep into the human psyche to find universal truths about how people want to live, lessons that warrant rediscovery especially by anyone who chooses to live in a small home in tune with nature.

Wright started out—as he finished—thinking small. His first house was the one he built in 1889 for himself and his wife, Catherine, in the Chicago suburb of Oak Park. With help from his mother, Anna, the twenty-two-year-old purchased a lot and then borrowed construction money from his employer, the noted architect Louis Sullivan (1856–1924). With Anna Wright's encouragement, emboldened by the Froebel blocks she gave him as a boy, Wright early on set his course for architecture. Although he left the University of Wisconsin after just one semester, his drafting skills had won him apprenticeships before he landed at the noted firm of Adler and Sullivan in 1888.

In shaping his own home, Wright nodded somewhat to tradition outside but began his domestic revolution inside. Most impressive were additions made in 1895 to the two-bedroom house, including a dining room whose furnishings were fully integrated into the architecture and an upstairs playroom for his growing brood that changed the definition of human scale. Reform, if not revolution, was in Chicago's air at the time. The city harbored myriad vocal proponents of housing reform, from social workers, labor leaders, and Arts and Crafts enthusiasts to feminists and ministers who urged that modern homes be simplified and beautified to achieve a rewarding family life.

Wright took up the cause of this movement to build "the house beautiful." As early as 1894 the young architect recommended simple houses with as few rooms as necessary. Those who plead small means, he lectured, "can never wash their sins away, for 'home' means more than money and the smaller means sometimes show the very best results.... The more simple the conditions become," he added, "the more careful you must be in the working out of your combinations in order that comfort and utility may go hand in hand with beauty as they inevitably should." For him architecture was a key tool of democratic societies such as America was trying to build, holding the power to accomplish social and political goals. These pronouncements were followed by volumes on the subject spoken and published over sixty-five years.

Among the earliest residences Wright designed were cottages and apartment houses, fueling his lifelong concern for getting "the very best results" from small quarters. For Louis Sullivan and one of the firm's Chicago clients, he added to his portfolio two vacation bungalows in Ocean Springs, Mississippi,

As historic photographs of the Stockman House document, the plan was more open than the typical house of the day (top). Wright used a massive brick fireplace in lieu of a wall to separate the living and dining areas. Beyond, both rooms flow outdoors onto a veranda. Another Wright innovation was to group windows together, as he did to flood the living area with light (above).

Among Wright's innovative early apartment projects were two in Milwaukee built in 1916, the Richards Duplexes (above) and the Munkwitz Duplexes (demolished in 1973). Both grew out of his efforts to design economical "ready-cut" residences, which he called American System-Built Homes. "Wright's interest went wherever possible beyond the ... individual building," commented the noted architectural historian Henry-Russell Hitchcock in 1942. " It was not his lack of interest, but society's lack of response that restricted his early development as a 'sociological' architect."

designed in 1890. Others followed after Wright left Sullivan's office and launched his own practice in 1893. These included open-plan summer retreats in the Great Lakes area, some of which were clad in horizontal board-and-batten siding that emphasized a home's relationship to the earth—what Wright saw as "the line of domesticity." In 1895 he produced three courtyard apartment complexes in Chicago encompassing one-, two-, and three-bedroom units: the Waller, Francisco Terrace, and Francis Apartments (the latter two demolished). Multifamily housing was a challenge he returned to, although several projects never made it off his drawing board.

The fame Wright earned with his own home was soon burnished with three designs for middle-class houses offered to *Ladies' Home Journal* readers in 1901 and 1907. The first, for "A Home in a Prairie Town," sealed the architect's position as the leader of the Prairie School. As important as the house was in establishing the tenets of Wright's Prairie style—windows banded together, sheltering eaves, a two-story living area, all tied to the earth—the accompanying "quadruple block plan" was even more groundbreaking. This proposal for optimal placement of residences to enhance both the houses and their neighborhood showed Wright's deep commitment to improving livability and the look of new suburban developments. He followed these remarkable ideas with "A Small House with 'Lots of Room in It'" and then in 1907 with "A Fireproof House for $5,000," Prairie houses that were were fleshed out in various commissions.

After a hiatus in Europe, where Wright escaped with his lover, Mamah Borthwick Cheney, in 1911 he began to pursue his vision of prefabricating homes to make them easier and cheaper to build. "Simply selling houses at less cost means nothing at all to me. To sell beautiful houses at less cost means everything," he said in 1916, adding that he wanted to deliver them "key in packet" (ready to move in). What he actually came up with, called the American System-Built Homes, were houses precut at the factory. Labeled pieces were shipped to the site to be erected according to Wright's plans, much like the mail-order bungalows then available from Sears and other suppliers. Wright developed dozens of designs for Arthur Richards and his partners in Milwaukee beginning in 1915, some costing as little as $2,750. Bungalows, one- and two-story houses (modeled after his "Fireproof House"), and apartments were built in the Milwaukee and Chicago areas before World War I put an end to the undertaking.

Wright persisted in trying to build residential utopias, making a start in 1915 with Ravine Bluffs in Glencoe, Illinois, a small project for his attorney, Sherman Booth. The next year he published a revised residential block plan to promote parklike suburbs offering both private and public spaces as picturesque as "the Gothic colleges of Oxford." Over the next two decades Wright channeled his planning ideas into an idealized proposal that he called Broadacre City. In this decentralized City of Tomorrow made possible by the automobile, each family—factory workers, professionals, farmers—would have a home and an acre of its own. Houses celebrating individual freedom, perhaps of steel and glass with prefabricated mechanical and plumbing units, would grow organically from the landscape.

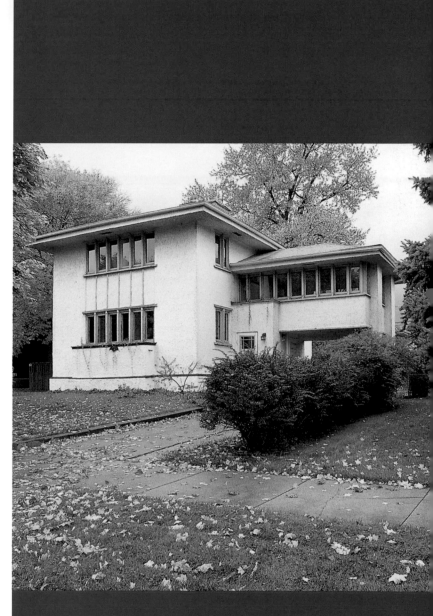

In addition to apartments, Wright also designed bungalows and two-story houses in conjunction with Arthur Richards's company. A number from 1916 and 1917 have been documented in Milwaukee and the Chicago area, such as one of the builder's model houses (above). This and others owe a debt to Wright's square-plan "Fireproof House for $5,000." Another example, the Wynant House (1916), was recently discovered in Gary, Indiana. In Atlantic City, New Jersey, casino revenues are paying for modern versions of Wright's American System designs—revived as affordable housing.

"The outside may come inside and the inside go outside," he suggested in his 1932 book *The Disappearing City.*

Wright never got to build Broadacre City, but he began constructing it house by house in the mid-1930s. All his ideas of how to build a moderate-cost home for the average home-owner culminated during the Great Depression in pared-down residences he called Usonians—architectural "citizens" of the United States of North America (Usonia to Wright's poetic mind). "There is nothing more interesting or more important in this world today," Wright told a 1939 gathering of British architects, "than trying to put into the houses in which our typical best citizens live something of the quality of a genuine work of art...."

Having to deal with material shortages and straitened times may have brought to mind the words of Thoreau: "Consider first how slight a shelter is absolutely necessary." Wright eliminated whatever he could: visible roofs, gutters and downspouts, attics and basements, garages, interior trim, plaster and paint, radiators, excessive furnishings. Materials were limited and repeated outside and in. A unit system setting a grid horizontally and vertically, like a cage, simplified construction. What was essential? A garden, for one, plus "a living room with as much garden coming into it as we can afford." A fireplace, a dining alcove near an efficient kitchen, with utilities behind, two bedrooms and a bathroom, perhaps a study, a carport.

Although the Jacobs House (1936) in Madison, Wisconsin, is considered Wright's first Usonian house, he himself found the seed for these efficiently built homes in his concrete-block designs constructed in Los Angeles in the early 1920s. The Jacobs family's home (opposite, top) clearly illustrates Wright's division of his Usonians into public and private sides. Walls rising to high clerestory windows keep out prying eyes on the public side (bottom left and right), while generous windows and French doors on the private side reach out to embrace nature (above). Even a tight Usonian budget was never too small for a Wright fireplace.

In 1938 Wright returned to his idea of "quadruple homes," creating an ingenious plan for sixteen homes in four units in Ardmore, Pennsylvania. Called Suntop Homes for the sunroof crowning each (top), the 2,300-square-foot homes were joined to save costs and allow as much surrounding garden as possible. Only one unit was built. The story was similar outside Lansing, Michigan, where only two houses came of Wright's 1939 plan for the Usonia I cooperative. Alma Goetsch and Katherine Winckler set off on their own, retaining the architect to design a house in Okemos (above) that is considered one of his best small Usonians.

The first Usonian house—with a little help from the owners, Katherine and Herbert Jacobs of Madison, Wisconsin—was produced for $5,500 in 1936. It became the theme, with 140 variations, of the last two decades of Wright's life. With its open plan, fewer personal possessions, freedom of movement yet privacy, Wright's Usonian template was anything but "another little imitation of a mansion." To him, as he said in 1938, "it seems a thing loving the ground with the new sense of space—light—and freedom to which our U.S.A. is entitled."

Over the next decade, bits and pieces of the Broadacre City concept came out of the closet, reduced and reconfigured as plans for middle-class communities of Usonian homes. The first, known as Usonia I, was proposed by professors at what is now Michigan State University in Lansing. Attempting to turn their food cooperative into a housing coop, they approached Wright in 1939. He designed seven homes surrounding a shared farm, but the group's bank loan was denied by the Federal Housing Authority, citing the "unusual design" of the houses.

Usonia Homes in Pleasantville, New York, fared better in the postwar economy and remains a thriving community after more than a half century. A coop of friends, incorporated in 1945, implored Wright to lay out their ninety-seven acres purchased two years later. His fifty-five circular lots, an acre apiece, had to be redesigned into more standard shapes to please the local zoning board. Wright, as agreed, designed just several houses and a community center; of these, only three of his designs were built, along with fifty houses by others, many designed by David Henken. At two other communities in Michigan planned around the same time—the Galesburg Country Homes and Parkwyn Village in Kalamazoo—only isolated Wright homes were built.

Yet Wright soldiered on in search of small-house solutions, reaching out to women in magazines such as *Life* and *House Beautiful* and to builders in *House and Home* and *Architectural Forum*. Whereas most of the early Usonians were supervised on site by Taliesin apprentices—beginning architects who studied at the Fellowship established by Wright and his wife, Olgivanna, in 1932—Wright in the 1950s decided to let owners build their own homes using a form of his concrete-block system developed in the 1920s. Some owners saved money, if not time, by casting blocks for their Usonian Automatics, but others called in a contractor. Beginning in 1956, a few prefabricated homes were also built.

In six decades spent trying to make the house of moderate cost every inch as satisfying as the mansion on the hill, Wright honed his concept of organic architecture—buildings that grow from nature. As he admitted in 1894, there are no "golden rules for house building," only "certain well-established principles." What follows on these pages, introducing profiles of nine of Wright's small wonders plus one created in his spirit, is a review of the principles that he himself spent a lifetime establishing. They provide wise counsel and inspiration for anyone contemplating the design or redesign of a home, small or large. Yet they are even more important in compact residences where every space consideration and every cost looms large.

How did Wright make a house of 1,200 square feet or so look bigger, feel spacious, and work better outside and in? He married the house to the ground, stretching it out under a broad roof

With just 870 square feet of living space, the Sturges House (1939) in Brentwood Heights, California, is one of Wright's smallest commissions (top). This Usonian cantilevers out over its hilly site to take in spectacular views, one of the techniques the architect used to make the most of a difficult site. Inside, he dispensed with a separate dining room, creating a compact dining nook as part of the living room (above). A built-in cabinet hides the kitchen without the need for a door. Inexpensive plywood chairs and tables take their places as extensions of the architecture.

epitomizing shelter. He sited it to naturally catch the sun and breezes as well as the best view. He used glass in place of solid materials and turned away from the street, guaranteeing privacy on the other side. He annexed the garden and distant vistas as outdoor rooms. He chose materials linked to the earth. He built in mystery in lieu of applying decoration. He experimented with systems for building better, faster, and cheaper.

Inside, Wright always kept the human form as his measure, using high ceilings but bringing them down to human scale with lower decks or features that fool the eye. He varied levels to playfully emphasize contrasts. He designed from inside out to avoid boxy rooms. He eliminated doors in the living area in favor of plans that wend their way around natural dividers, expanding vistas inside as well as outside. He moved the dining room into the living area, providing easy access to outdoor terraces. He designed built-ins to save space, even lining his few hallways with cabinets or bookcases. He viewed other furnishings as part of the whole, seamlessly uniting materials, colors, and textures to achieve a sense of harmony and repose.

"I believe a house is more a home by being a work of Art," wrote Wright in *The Natural House* in 1954, summing up his principles. He advised others to copy those guidelines—not his architecture—urging that buildings be a product of their own time. Any home so conceived will sit more lightly on the land than the modern-day castles sprouting up on our farmland— hardly Wright's idea of organic architecture. As the owners of the Wright houses on the following pages themselves testify, small remains infinitely more rewarding.

With houses such as the Cass residence on Staten Island, New York (opposite, top and bottom left), and the Rudin House in Madison, Wisconsin (bottom right), Wright revived his hopes for prefabrication. The two, dating from 1959 and 1957, respectively, show different designs created for the developer Marshall Erdman. None of the dozen built proved to be as low cost as Wright planned. In 1953 he brought his residential visions to a wide audience with a 1,700-square-foot model Usonian home (top) built on the present site of the Guggenheim Museum in New York City. On a visit with his clients Roland and Ronny Reisley at Usonia Homes in Pleasantville, New York, Wright in 1952 took time out to redraw a fireplace grate (above). "After fifty years," says Roland Reisley, "I have realized that there was not a single day when I did not see something beautiful in the space around me."

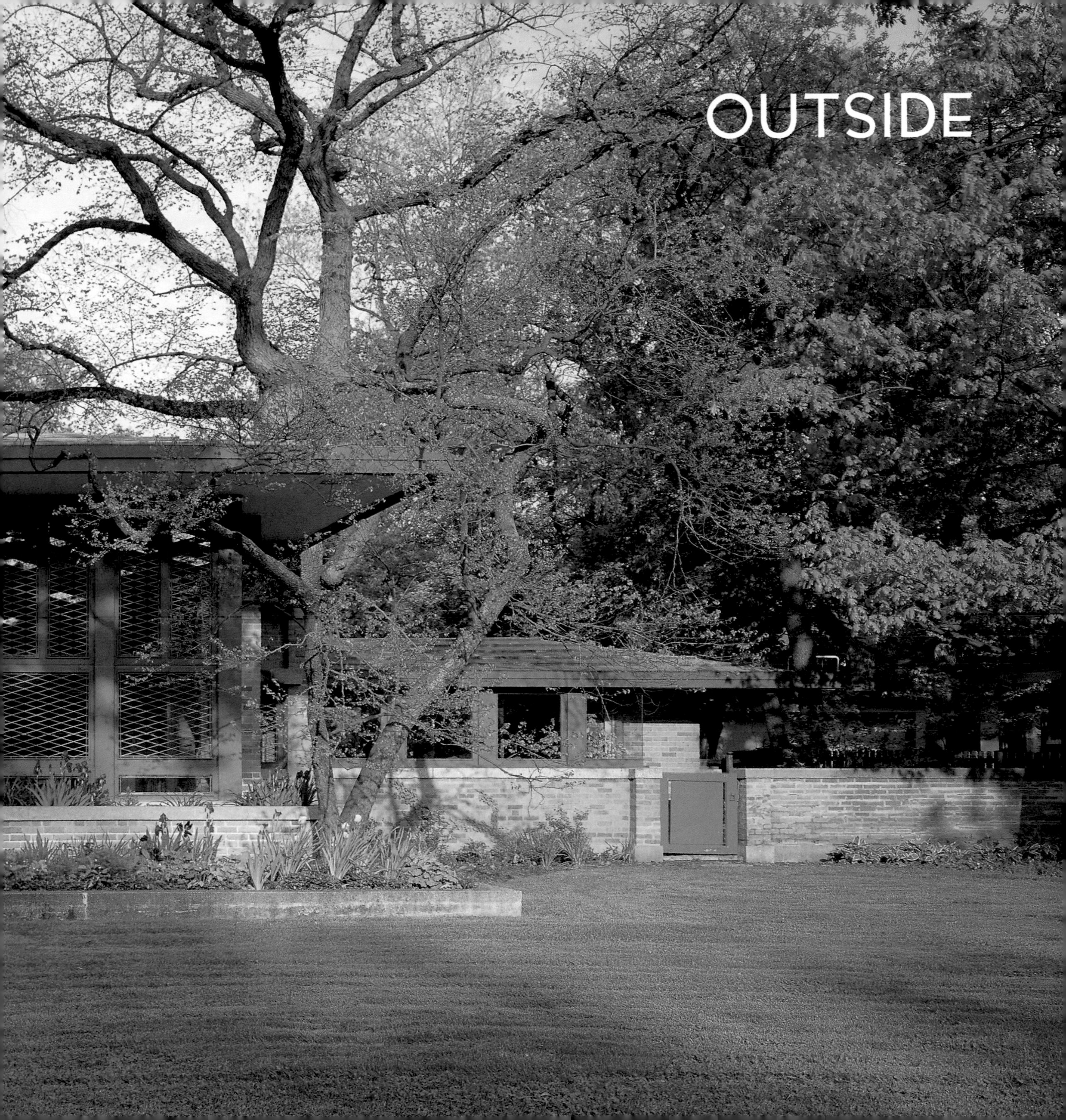
OUTSIDE

One only has to conjure up a mental image of Fallingwater to understand that Wright took delight in designing for sites where no one else wanted to—or could—build. But not every lot comes with a waterfall or a ravine or a dramatic hill, and not all homeowners have a pocketbook to match that of Liliane and Edgar Kaufmann, his clients at Fallingwater (1935). "With a small budget the best kind of land to build on is flat land," Wright wrote in *The Natural House* (1954). "Of course," he added, "if you can get a gentle slope, the building will be more interesting, more satisfactory."

Slope or no slope, Wright let the land speak for itself. For him architecture began with the site, its character dictating what would rise from it. A home, he said, should appear to grow organically from its site like a tree from the soil, built of the hill, not on it, and giving few hints where the ground leaves off and the building begins. It should be a "companion to the horizon." In nature Wright saw the freedom of America itself.

He designed his houses to suit the site rather than change the site to suit the house. The first steps were to capture the sun and find a property's trees and vistas, building in a way that preserved a view of these features from inside. To save money Wright built parallel with the land's contours. If this resulted in placement of a house at an angle to the street, all the better to avoid pushing up against lot lines and feeling cramped. A Wrightian house, set back on its lot, also wrapped itself around the landscape with walls and terraces that naturally insinuated themselves right into nature. "As a result," said *House Beautiful* in October 1959, "his houses seem as big as the outdoors."

THE SITE

Build with the land to capture light and views

For Wright, a large lot was not necessary—only a large vision. Eleanor Oboler's one-room studio (1940) in Malibu, California, takes in a view far greater than its size (above). Like a tree house held aloft on a trunk of rubblestone, the aerie is anchored to the earth even as it rises gently above it. At the Walker House (1949) in Carmel, California, Wright listened to the sea instead of the earth (opposite). Above the stone prow, as sandy as the shoreline, a captain's bridge of glass projects the living room seaward. The window wall of the house, originally 1,200 square feet, cuts a 180-degree arc and is stepped out to enlarge the view from inside. Six-foot eaves serve as a sun visor—or an umbrella when it rains.

THE HORIZONTAL LINE

Stress horizontals for a sense of spaciousness

Wright famously declared in 1910 that the "horizontal line is the line of domesticity." Houses should be "married to the ground," said this architect of the prairie. There features as varied as the limbs of trees and layers of rock scribe their own natural horizontal lines above and below the land's own "quiet level." The tradeoff for eliminating unnecessary height, for being closer to the earth, is a more intimate relationship with nature.

Architectural techniques Wright used heightened every house's sense of shelter while extracting every visual inch from small residences. He first eliminated basements so that his houses could begin on the ground, not in it with an unused damp cellar. Instead he placed each house on a foundation—a platform—marked with a base course to emphasize where it began, wedding it to the earth. Horizontal planes, which he called "the

true earth-line of human life, indicative of freedom," were stressed with bands of dark wood on light stucco or rows of siding parallel to the ground. Mortar between courses of brick was raked to emphasize the horizontal, and vertical joints were colored to match and troweled flush to minimize their importance.

Rooflines and cantilevers seemingly extending to infinity, "a quiet skyline" marked only by a low chimney, connected bands of windows, broad terraces, and outreaching walls all reinforced Wright's preferred line—a "new sense of repose" that identifies his work. "His horizontal rhythms," notes Donald Hoffman in *Frank Lloyd Wright: Architecture and Nature,* "told the truth of things by expressing the repose of masses in harmony with gravity and the landscape; his architecture spoke of life here and now, not the kingdom of a Christian heaven."

Wright would have liked how snow simplifies the landscape surrounding Sara and Melvyn Maxwell Smith's house in Bloomfield Hills, Michigan, outlining its overriding horizontality. Designed in 1946 but not completed until 1950, the three-bedroom house was a typical L-shaped Usonian whose bedroom wing was enlarged by Taliesin Associated Architects in 1970. The line of the broad projecting roofs is carried even farther forward by a low terrace wall; board-and-batten siding and a wall of windows strengthen the streamlined effect, with a vertical wall the only counterpoint.

Nature was Wright's teacher in so many ways, few of them as important as its lesson on cantilevering. Birds do it, trees do it, layers of rock striated by upheavals do it. Wings, branches, and masonry shelves all stretch out in flights of freedom, breaking boundaries. It did not take Wright long to see the spatial benefits of similarly releasing buildings from their traditional walled confines. With cantilevers he let them soar like a bird on the wing or a branch swaying in the wind.

The cantilever, an architectural projection reaching well beyond its base of support, was Wright's chief tool for holding the horizontal line. Its benefit to small houses is obvious: a cantilever visually expands a structure beyond its own footprint, adding space in the air that does not have to be built on the ground. Wright used cantilevers in dramatically overhanging rooflines, elevated terraces and balconies, walls, trim, even planters. These series of horizontal planes created layers as intricate as the limbs, branches, twigs, and leaves of the trees that inspired them.

Wright described his cantilevers as a waiter's tray resting on upturned fingers. Removing supporting posts at the corners "in favor of structural continuity," they put an end to post-and-beam construction for him. He was met with initial resistance: "Walls made one with floors and ceilings, merging together yet reacting upon each other, the engineer had never met." The emergence of steel and reinforced concrete for support made cantilevers more feasible, but he also built them of wood, stone, and brick. For Wright, the cantilever's possibilities were among the most compelling in all of architecture. As he said in *The Natural House,* "It can do remarkable things to liberate space."

CANTILEVERS
Design dramatic overhangs to symbolize freedom

Seemingly without support, outstretched roofs cantilever over the master bedroom and the porch of the Mary Adams House (1905) in Highland Park, Illinois (opposite). At the Tomek House (1907) in Riverside, Illinois, precursors of Wright's seminal Robie House (1908) are in evidence (above). All that remains of the corner posts are vestiges cut off halfway up, letting the eye fill in the space now liberated. Limestone lintels themselves cantilever over the stucco walls. Above sits an equally cantilevered planter.

27

ROOFS

Stretch the roofline parallel to the ground

In the 1908 Prairie house designed for Sophie and Meyer May in Grand Rapids, Michigan, the roofs seem poised for takeoff. Clad in red tile, they intersect in a complex ode to shelter. Two front overhangs shade an upstairs balcony and a lower veranda, while a veranda to the side has its own protection. Light-colored eaves direct sunlight inside. Closer to the ground, the foundation and window sills perform a horizontal zigzag to match.

Wright began his architectural revolution at the top. The roof embodied his conception of a house "as livable interior space under ample shelter. I liked the sense of shelter in the look of the building," he recalled in 1954. What is a house for except shelter— keeping out the elements, shading the sun, and deflecting moisture? Wright tended to recess the walls into the background, like modestly retiring Japanese shoji screens underneath a strong roof, letting a house's cap determine its character.

By eliminating the attic, he kept roofs low and thus in league with the ground—maintaining the horizontal line even

when his roofs sometimes stepped upward to accommodate a slope or a hillside. Continuing the prairie metaphor, exaggerated eaves hover overhead to stress the idea of shelter. The flat undersides reflect diffused light back into the windows below. Where overhangs might keep winter sun away, walls were pushed outward.

Even as Wright moved from low gabled to hipped and then flat designs, he used the roof to make all his houses look bigger. It stretches out well beyond the interior confines, sometimes occupying double the floor space. Overhangs of three to ten feet expand the house's footprint accordingly. Deep fascias outline the outward thrust as if pointing to nature. A low roofline at the front heeds human scale but appears higher when the building is longer. The roof covers all in one swoop, eliminating the need for separate entrance canopies and providing a frame for built-in features such as a trellis. "No dormers nor any excrescences. No saw-tooth upheavals...," Wright had ordered in 1896. By 1955 he declared: "In the way the walls rose from the plan and the spaces were roofed over was the chief interest of the house."

CHIMNEYS

Avoid an undersized chimney on a big roof

Stanley and Mildred Rosenbaum's 1939 Usonian house in Florence, Alabama, came with two broad brick chimneys, reflecting brick fireplaces in the living room and the study. Carefully integrated into the overall L-shaped design, they add a small vertical counterpoint that causes the house's horizontal lines to seem even larger. In Usonian houses this masonry core typically serves as a pivot point around which the kitchen and utilities are arranged.

When Wright began his career at the end of the nineteenth century, all he could see atop "distorted roof surfaces" of Victorian houses were tall, thin chimneys bristling up from "tortured skylines"—to him they looked like "sooty fingers threatening the sky." His solution was one or at most two broad, generous chimneys, low like his gently sloping or flat roofs. He kept the horizontal line of the earth in view.

A substantial chimney was the outward manifestation of the hearth inside, the heart of the home. It promised the warmth of family life around a real fireplace, not merely a mantel serving as "a marble frame for a few coals in a grate." Wright liked to face his fireplaces in the same stone or brick used for the chimneys, striving for a seamless unity of materials inside and out. Chimneys were an integral piece of the design, never an afterthought. A short vertical punctuation mark on the horizontal line, they anchor their houses to the ground.

Front doors of Wright houses do not usually call out to visitors, who are gently taken in hand on a little voyage of discovery. Down a walkway, turn right, turn left, up the steps, turn again— the architect makes us work to uncover his grand scheme. Tucked under a broad overhanging roof or a cantilevered balcony, the entrance beckons from the shadows. Mystery is the secret ingredient in this game of finding one's way through the maze, out of the dark and into the light.

Wright railed against houses that had only "an especially ugly hole to go in and come out of." A tiny entrance would be lost on a wide expanse of wall, he reasoned, whereas a large entrance seemed proportionally even grander. French doors used at entrances broaden the opening into a natural void in a solid wall. Other Wrightian entries are sculpted out of the facade or hidden on the side. Each one stars in an architectural drama whereby one moves from the public world to the private one inside.

ENTRANCES

Properly scale the entrance and add mystery

At Kentuck Knob (1954) in Chalkhill, Pennsylvania, broad steps reach out to heighten the sense of arrival. Rather than use the doorway merely to separate outside and in, Wright carved a screen of light into the rustic sandstone walls to mark the point of entry. Sequestered beneath the eaves in the arc of the angle, its low scale bids a quiet welcome. A split-stone chimney offers a hint of the matching floor-to-ceiling fireplace found just inside.

NATURAL
MATERIALS

Tie a house to the earth with wood or masonry

Kin to the turning sumac outside, this early Usonian house in Bloomfield Hills, Michigan, is natural in every way. A cantilevered terrace seems to touch the forest from which its own lapped cypress boards came, their horizontal lines mimicking the neat pattern of the sumac. Gregor and Elizabeth Affleck, inspired by Fallingwater, had Wright design this house over a ravine in 1941. Past the trellis and inside a glass-covered loggia, a stream flows by in clear view from a hatch that brings nature right indoors.

"Every material has its own eloquent message, its own lyrical song, and no one has made them sing so beautifully as Frank Lloyd Wright," observed Robert Mosher, one of Wright's Taliesin apprentices, in a November 1955 *House Beautiful* issue on his mentor. Wright preferred natural building materials, used them naturally, and repeated the same materials outside and in to create symphonies as perfectly composed as any by Beethoven. Their natural colors—the bosky browns of wood, the fiery reds of brick, the earthy grays and tans of stone, the neutral hues of concrete—became "the architect's garden," as he called it. Applied ornament was thrown out with the paint cans.

Wright found treasure without end buried in the earth. Wood was his favorite, whether oak, cypress, or Philippine mahogany; board-and-batten, clapboard, or plywood; waxed or oiled or perhaps stained to bring up the true nature of the materials. "I learned to see wood as wood," he explained in 1954, refusing to carve it or force it into unnatural acts. Stone was another top choice, preferably a rustic example such as sandstone or limestone laid as it came from the quarry. It suited houses in the country, as did brick for urban commissions; flat, narrow Roman brick hewed to his horizontal line. Concrete, architecture's "despised outcast," was woven into blocks imprinted like textiles.

For each house one material set a simple theme that was reinforced by minor variations, a choice that helps streamline small residences. By using natural materials, naturally colored, Wright could be accused of making modest houses recede into the background. But by heeding their surroundings, they earn what he saw as the larger reward of architectural honesty.

WALLS

Use walls as screens to free outside and inside

"America was born to destroy the facade in all things, governmental or personal, that do not express the inner spirit," Wright told readers of *House Beautiful* in July 1953. He did his part to change the look of houses, letting the enclosed space within dictate the outward appearance—not the other way around, as previous architecture had done. The evolution in his own thinking about walls occurred when he "began to see a building primarily not as a cave but as broad shelter in the open, related to vista; vista without and vista within."

Wright started by figuratively tearing down walls, tossing

The Thomas House (1901) was one of Wright's first Prairie houses and the first to be built in Oak Park, just down the street from the architect's own home. With this design he succeeded in banishing the box that most people called home. A house no longer had to be seen as just four straight walls with holes cut out for windows and doors. Walls rise up only to a high sill level, where windows have been grouped together for maximum impact. Lighted at night, the wall seems to vanish, leaving the roofs to float ethereally above.

out the concept of a wall as the side of a box in which holes are punched. Once he saw walls not as an impediment to light and air but as the enclosure of space, he began to bring them "towards the function of a screen." Out went the artistic rigidity of post-and-beam construction and in came the freedom to open corners with cantilevers and to replace solid walls with clear glass. The whole wall could then be used as a palette without affecting structural stability. Exterior finishes gained the plasticity of flesh on bones, the "expressive flow of continuous surface."

In his Prairie houses Wright began organizing walls into long courses that reinforced the horizontal plane, making them loom larger in the landscape. For two-story designs, he let the upper band of windows naturally divide the wall at the sill line and pushed the windows up under the eaves to replace the cornice. By the time he began experimenting with uniform-sized concrete blocks in the 1920s and then moved on to Usonian houses in the 1930s, he had mastered how to keep walls from being barriers and instead sculpted his facades to express the space inside.

WINDOWS

Don't simply punch holes in a wall for windows

From the outside Wright's windows are, as he forecast in 1896, "indicative of good cheer and brightness within." By the time he was designing Usonians such as the Goetsch-Winckler House (1939) in Okemos, Michigan, he was proficient at building in light with airy window walls (above). Even at the early Davidson House (1908) in Buffalo, New York, light replaces the solidity of walls (opposite). Wright's aim was to take "the corners out, put in glass instead."

Wright's favorite building material was probably glass, a "magic material, there but not seen," he said in 1928. "I suppose as a material we may regard it as crystal—thin sheets of air in air to keep air out or keep it in." Glass was his ally in breaking down the solidity of traditional walls. In their place he put expansive bands of windows, which he called "light screens."

"Fewer window holes though much greater window area" became Wright's dictum. By grouping windows to suit each room's needs, he gained unity, simplicity, and broad views that single holes cut randomly out of a wall could never provide. He insisted on a casement window that swings outward toward nature. "If it had not existed I should have invented it," he said in 1954.

Seeing windows as screens filtering light, it became natural to etch them with geometric and stylized nature designs that stencilled patterns on the walls and floors inside. Strands of these translucent ribbons, framed between dark lintels and sills, made walls seem to disappear beneath their floating roofs above. For the later Usonian houses, built when art glass was too labor intensive, Wright simply exploded the size and extent of windows, using wood frames that made their own decoration.

Window walls stretching from floor to ceiling turn small houses from boxes—caves—into roofed shelters that invite nature inside. Glass French doors, like casement windows, also become screens, folding in and out to touch the outdoors. Windows mitered at the corner make walls completely vanish, increasing the feeling of spaciousness inside. "Glass alone, with no help from any of us," said Wright in 1931, "would eventually have destroyed classic architecture, root and branch."

Geometry—nature's organization—underlies all of Wright's work. It is the grammar with which his buildings speak, learned from flowers, honeycombs, crystals, and other symbols of life itself. Wright used this grammar to form his own design language, beginning with a unit system for building. He often likened himself to a weaver who fabricated architecture just as a rug's pile is stitched into the warp. He wove tapestries of interdependent units, first based on squares and cubes and then on circles and more complex forms such as hexagons and ellipses.

Standardization as found in nature signified order, unity, and beauty for Wright. He relied on it to set a grid for his designs that might determine the dimensions of the materials used—such as molded concrete blocks—or was itself determined by a material—such as the two-by-fours used in Usonian houses. These later houses, launched in tough economic times, aimed to eliminate on-site labor and erect the outside and inside walls in one step. Wright expanded the grid planning of his Prairie houses, using a vertical module sized at one foot, one inch and a two-by-four horizontal unit system based on materials such as plywood. This produced a framework akin to a cage in which everything would fit uniformly and thus less expensively.

Although short of true prefabrication, walls for the early Usonians were shipped from the factory for easy assembly on site. Heating, lighting, and plumbing systems were consolidated for easy installation. Wright also saved his clients money by paring his palette of materials to maybe three or five. In the name of economy, plasterers and painters were shunned, along with gutters, downspouts, basements, and ornamental trim.

STANDARDIZED COMPONENTS

Economize on construction and materials

Two-by-four-foot board-and-batten siding helped determine the grid system for the first Jacobs House (1936) in Madison, Wisconsin (opposite). Wright's planning modules saved money by simplifying the construction process, which was further streamlined by limiting materials to wood, brick, glass, and concrete. Pine with redwood battens supplies built-in color and pattern. For his "textile-block" designs such as the Freeman House (1923) in Los Angeles, Wright created his own material from scratch (above). The self-styled weaver embedded pattern in molded concrete blocks that were stacked to form the walls outside and in. Mitered glass turns walls into a disappearing act. Marked off in simple rectangles, the glass seamlessly reflects the concrete blocks themselves.

PRIVATE SPACES

Create a private side, away from the street

At the residence of Ray and Mimi Brandes, built in 1952 in the Seattle suburb of Issaquah, Washington, the facade (above, left) is more open than many of Wright's Usonians. An elevated band of windows on the office-workshop end is paired beyond the carport with French doors leading into the entrance loggia. The flagstone patio in front was a rare concession to the house's isolated setting. On its private side, tall doors open the living area and bedrooms onto a secluded terrace, which is encircled with a retaining wall whose rosy concrete blocks match those of the house (above, right).

For Wright and others who came of age during the housing reform movement at the turn of the twentieth century, the family reigned as the preeminent social unit. Home took on a role of refuge from urban life, a spiritual as well as a physical haven from the encroaching industrial society. "Make the whole world homelike," declared Frances Willard, the temperance leader. To shut out distractions, Wright turned his attention to the back of the house, where privacy could be built in.

Even in his early Prairie houses, Wright directed his clients' lives inward. Interior courtyards, such as the one he built at

his own Taliesin (1911–59) in Spring Green, Wisconsin, allowed families to relax beyond the peering eyes of neighbors. His scintillating art glass windows offered additional privacy without the need for curtains. Their geometric patterns were adroitly arranged around clear glass to keep unwanted gazes to a minimum.

The Usonian designs of the mid-1930s to the late 1950s recognized that small suburban houses had to guard their privacy. As families retreated further indoors, the face turned to the street was somewhat more austere. High windows on a solid wall and narrow clerestories above convey a sense of protection on the exterior. But the front door opens into an explosion of space, light, and freedom: walls of glass and patio doors on the opposite side usher in natural light, open plans offer wide-open views that do not stop at blocky walls, and natural materials and earthy colors create a seamless link with nature. These houses are two-sided, open and closed. On one side is the outside world, held at bay by boards or bricks and mortar; on the other side, unleashed by window walls, is a totally private interior universe.

Although homeowners are rediscovering the joys of the front porch, Wright was never a big fan of porches. "That curse of the American home" he called any such appendage blocking sunlight from the interior. Wright instead annexed the great outdoors, giving his houses one or more open-air rooms: a walled terrace or an open patio perhaps, or roofed verandas, balconies, or garden pavilions. In addition to taking in sights beyond the property line through generous windows, extending the floor plan into outdoor rooms was a boon for Wright's smaller commissions.

Inspired by nature, Wright reached out to embrace it architecturally. Long, low garden walls extend the horizontal line into the landscape, taking the house's building materials with them. Attached verandas, as Wright specified in 1896, are "a summery, good-time place ... so arranged as to be enclosed and not a common walkway for those coming and going to the house." Balconies, first tested in the Prairie era and then perfected at Fallingwater, thrust a house into the outdoors. Wright did not forget nature's mirrors: water features such as pools reflected back the architecture, doubling its effect while adding coolness; gurgling fountains played music in the landscape.

A modest Prairie house typically has an enclosed terrace or two, hidden at the side or front behind a low wall. Usonian living areas open onto a concrete or paved terrace that may continue around the bedrooms to put them in touch with nature as well. More extensive surrounding terraces of brick or stone visually enlarge a house beyond its actual square footage, demolishing one more barrier between humans and nature.

OUTDOOR ROOMS

Bring the outside in with terraces and balconies

The Scottsdale, Arizona, residence of Bruce Brooks Pfeiffer—a short walk from Wright's desert home, Taliesin West (1937–59)—takes advantage of the climate to stretch the idea of shelter. In 1971 Pfeiffer adapted the unbuilt 1938 plan for the Jester House, using stucco instead of wood. Indoor spaces merge into outdoor rooms with an ease possible in few other climates. A river of red concrete connects a series of circular living pavilions (opposite, top). Using the living room (bottom) requires a walk outdoors, albeit sheltered. A round pool (above) offers more than just a mirage.

LANDSCAPES

Plant native materials to complement the house

**Soon after Mary and William Palmer moved into their 1950 Uson-
ian in Ann Arbor, Michigan (above), they began to hone its wooded
landscape. Broad steps make a gentle transition to the outdoors.
Avid gardeners, the Palmers planted pines, English yews, holly,
dogwood, ferns, daylilies, liriope, and ground covers. Bulbs and
woodland flowers outline bark-lined paths and a dry stream that
meander through the property (opposite, top left and right). The
couple's love of Japanese culture can be seen in an eighteenth-
century stone lantern (bottom left) and a teahouse designed in
1964 by John Howe, a former Wright apprentice (bottom right).**

Trees, flowers, plants—Wright aspired to make his buildings as
organic as these creations of nature, unearthing in their cells
a geometric blueprint for his architecture. Summers spent
working in the fields of Wisconsin as a boy and lessons learned
from Emerson, Thoreau, and Whitman filled him with a lifelong
respect for nature. It was his teacher, his church. When it came
to creating landscapes for his own designs, he rejected Victorian extravaganzas such as foundation plantings, parterres, and
evergreens clipped in unnatural shapes.

Instead Wright stressed natural materials naturally planted,
simplified as in a Japanese print or garden so that "you couldn't
tell where the architecture leaves off and the garden begins."
His landscape principles make even small residences feel like
country estates. Borrowing distant scenery—trees, stones, water, mountains—instantly enlarges any property. Exposing the
foundation to show where it meets the ground focuses attention on the building. Setting the house back on its lot and using plantings as buffers increase the sense of privacy. Raising
a house ensures exceptional views no matter its size.

A Wrightian landscape uses native trees and shrubs to eliminate excessive watering and care. Key trees are saved, not cut
down, and foliage is massed as it grows naturally. Perennials
screen, shade, and separate spaces. Planters overflowing with
trailing vines stress the earth's gravity and natural bounty. Trel-
lises connect a house to the land while stenciling patterns beneath. Window boxes call attention to their windows above.
Lawns, like a platter, underscore the horizontal line. The garden
is designed to complement, not compete with, the architecture.

CARPORTS

Build a carport to extend the line of the house

The open road symbolized freedom to Wright, a lover of fast cars. When the motor was off, nothing short of an architectural symbol to match would do to house the car. Early in his career he gave the owners of his large Prairie houses garages for their new toys, some discreetly retired to a basement level. Within a few decades, however, he grew to dislike the garage's "gaping hole."

As Wright began searching for ways to save his clients money in the 1930s, he took the traditional porte cochere—shelter for the age of horses and buggies—and extended it into an off-street port for "the now inevitable car." Doing away with a garage's four walls, he invented a sleek carport typically cantilevered out from the entry, kitchen, or another supporting wall as much as eighteen feet. Like a hand extended in welcome, it offered shelter at less cost while daringly projecting the horizontal line into space. By siting the house toward the back of the property, Wright gained yet another way to add drama with a long driveway and an entry court echoing the architectural grid.

The carport at the Rosenbaum House in Alabama, built as part of the entry, easily converted the L-shaped Usonian design into a T. An architecture critic who saw a photograph of it in 1940 compared the carport to a "great bird in flight." Carports worked less well in northern climates such as Wisconsin and Michigan, where these experimental flying appendages tended to sag a bit under the weather. Wright also designed a circular freestanding carport.

Like any living thing, Wright's organic buildings were designed to grow. Change did not bother him—in fact, he encouraged it and planned for it in his Usonian houses. He regarded them as "polliwogs," or tadpoles with a tail that might start out short and then grow long. The tail end of the house was the bedroom wing, set apart in its own quiet zone.

Small Usonians typically had two or three bedrooms, so this was a logical place to expand as children of young families grew older. To Wright these houses were "an ideal breeding stable." He went back to the Rosenbaum House in Alabama in 1948, a decade after it was built, to add a boys' dormitory and a guest room fronting a Japanese garden, with a hallway in between. Other homeowners followed suit, extending their polliwog tail or moving non-weight-bearing walls installed to facilitate the inevitable. Using the same planning grid, form, and materials as the originals, the additions look as if they had always been there.

ADDITIONS
Expand when a house becomes too small

When Wright in 1951 sketched out a home for Roland and Ronny Reisley at Usonia Homes in Pleasantville, New York, two bedrooms facing the balcony here seemed enough. Before long they felt an acute need for more space as their family grew. Wright obliged with a 120-degree addition beyond the living-dining area at right, housing three bedrooms, a bath, and a playroom. The striking cantilevered carport on the left shelters the entry, beside the kitchen.

INSIDE

"Unity was their watchword, the sign and symbol that thrilled them, the Unity of all things!" Wright wrote in his 1932 autobiography about his family, which included Unitarians and a number of preachers. Lessons such as this learned at his mother's knee emerged later as part of Wright's philosophy of organic architecture. For him, buildings that grow from the earth express a oneness with nature, a unity with all of the world's living things.

In unity he saw integrity and truth ("Truth against the world" was the motto of his Lloyd Jones ancestors). How did he translate this into architecture? By developing a unifying grammar for each building, the language through which it speaks in one voice. Wright's geometric vocabulary was a system as orderly as the cells of a plant. He used modules—squares, rectangles, triangles, hexagons, parallelograms, circles, ellipses—to determine a floor plan and shape space both horizontally and vertically. This central idea extended to all the details, integral ornament, and furnishings. The result, as he said in 1908, is that "each building aesthetically is cut from one piece of goods and consistently hangs together with an integrity impossible otherwise."

A unified design idea edits a small house by avoiding competing styles—following the rules of grammar. "Consistency from first to last will give you the result you seek and consistency alone," Wright preached as early as 1894. "Not sensation, not show, not meaningless carpenter work and vulgar decoration, but quiet thoughtful consistency throughout...."

UNITY

Base the design on one central idea

Virginia and Donald Lovness's 1955 home is based on a four-foot-square module, a motif that unifies every aspect of its design. In the living room of their Stillwater, Minnesota, residence (opposite), the square is inscribed in the red concrete floor and echoed in the square red cushions of the furniture they made themselves. Square tables, square chair backs, and cascading squares forming the Taliesin lamp in the background (above) all pick up the theme, as do blocks in the limestone walls and the massive hearth.

As Wright was designing his groundbreaking Unity Temple in his hometown of Oak Park in 1905, he had an epiphany: "The enclosed space within ... is the *reality* of the building." He discovered that the interior space—not exterior walls or the roof—should dictate a building's outward appearance. From then on he tried to let the rooms inside shape the architecture according to the needs of the occupants. He rejected classical styles as "tombs of a life that has been lived," as design dictators making interiors conform to old ideas of what a building should look like.

S P A C E

Design a house from the inside out

The Goetsch-Winckler House (1939) in Okemos, Michigan, was meant to be part of Wright's first community of Usonian houses, a project that fell victim to timid financiers. Alma Goetsch and Katherine Winckler, however, boldly proceeded with their innovative house. A book-lined reading alcove off the living area pushes outward beyond the compact kitchen, which is set apart only by the brick wall holding the fireplace. The dining table projecting from that wall and a short wall marking the kitchen act as natural dividers, creating an entry area inside the glass front doors.

Wright set out to change traditional cut-up interiors: "boxes beside boxes or inside boxes, called *rooms* ... cellular sequestration that implied ancestors familiar with penal institutions," as he mordantly described them in 1954. He let his rooms project outward as they needed to, using cruciform and L shapes to destroy the old square box for living. He began to see a house as shelter creating vistas within while capturing them outside. Except in sleeping areas, he eliminated doors and partitions, molding continuous space freed by the removal of posts, columns, corners, and thresholds. As spaces began to unfold gently, boring right angles were banished from Wright's vocabulary.

By doing away with interior walls or using short walls and screens—see-through walls—living areas offer up views from one end of a house to the other, creating a new sense of space. Strategic placement of built-ins and furnishings bends vistas around natural dividers, adding a touch of mystery. In a Wrightian design, the focus changes from what the neighbors think of the exterior to how the residents experience their own house inside.

In reshaping the modern interior, Wright mediated between the desire for liberating space and the basic human need for shelter and privacy. With his Prairie houses he began to see the first floor as essentially one large room, with different activity areas screened off. Gone were stuffy, unused parlors, a warren of hallways lined with doors, and ostentatious open staircases. In their place came free-flowing, often asymmetrical spaces that architecturally united family members.

The Prairie plans tended to be cruciform or pinwheel in shape, their quartet of arms holding living room, dining room, kitchen, and reception area downstairs and bedrooms and bathroom upstairs. By moving circulation space away from the center, to the outer edge, Wright was able to relocate the fireplace from the outside wall to the heart of the house. There it became a pivot point from which all space emanated. The dining room was "so coupled with the living room that one leads naturally into the other without destroying the privacy of either," he said in 1901.

As Wright tackled the problem of small houses with his Usonians in the 1930s, he changed the old cruciform into a sleeker L shape governed by a geometric unit system. Bedrooms came downstairs, tucked into their own quiet zone in one part of the ell. In the other leg, the dining room was remade into a "sunny alcove" of the living area. The kitchen at the conjunction became a compact "workspace" within sight of the family. While glass walls framed wide views outside, these open plans used oblique angles to create an interior landscape of seemingly unlimited vistas. As Wright found, substituting irregular planes for boxy rooms confuses spatial boundaries, visually enlarging the space.

OPEN PLANS
Substitute free-flowing spaces for boxy rooms

On the ground floor of the two-story May House (1908) in Grand Rapids, Michigan, spaces flow effortlessly into one another. The living room (opposite) is separated from the entry behind a low bookcase wall whose wood screen filters light into the room. Beyond, another partial wall bearing a flowered mural divides the dining room from the gallery leading to a front veranda. Without solid walls to intervene, sightlines meander from point to point (above). Bands of wood, like ribbons, tie together all the spaces.

HUMAN SCALE

Size interior spaces to avoid intimidation

Wright usually criticized artwork "hung in effigy upon the walls"— protesting that his architecture was art enough—but for the 1946 house in Tacoma, Washington, that he designed for Chauncey and Johanna Griggs, he made an exception. A gallery thirty-five feet long and fourteen feet wide, opened up with a wall of glass at left leading to the terrace, was created so that the owners could display their collections. The soaring ceiling with its abstract forest of trusses might have seemed intimidating if Wright had not brought it down to human scale. The trusses rest on a narrow deck—a false ceiling—holding recessed lighting. Warmed by the light and the small scale of the board-and-batten wall, the space manages to combine both freedom and a comforting sense of intimacy.

"Without a sense of proportion, no one should attempt to build," Wright admonished in 1928 in one of a series of articles he wrote for *Architectural Record.* Proportion came naturally to him, kept in check by the plan and the unit system chosen for each house. At the heart of proportion was scale—human scale, a term that Wright is said to have coined. The human beings for whom buildings are built were his constant measure. "Wright was perhaps more attentive to and accomplished in the adjustment of spaces to the human scale than any other architect in modern times," suggests Robert McCarter in *Frank Lloyd Wright: A Primer on Architectural Principles.*

"In the matter of scale," Wright explained, "the human being is the logical norm because buildings are to be humanly inhabited and should be related to human proportions not only comfortably but agreeably. People should belong to the building just as it should belong to them." The human scale Wright used tended to be his own height: five feet, eight inches.

Different spaces call out for different scales. In an area where one is seated, such as in the dining room or a reading nook, a low ceiling stresses the sense of enclosure. A raised ceiling over an area where one is standing or walking, such as the center of the living room, feels more in proportion to the body's full height. People also experience spaces differently as they move around. Wright lowered his fireplace openings and mantels, allowing residents a feeling of comparative power as they sat near the hearth or, on rising from a seated position, towered above it. "Human beings," cautioned Wright, "should look as well in the building or of it as flowers do."

FOYERS

Create an entry to shield the living area

Wright's entrances were no more boxes than his houses themselves. At the Bazett-Frank House (1939) in Hillsborough, California, an early Usonian, the foyer is open to possibility. Down the stairs is the living-dining area, outside awaits one of three terraces, and to the right lie the bedrooms. Compressed space here gives way to an uplifted ceiling in the living room. Even in this 1,500-square-foot residence, designed on a hexagonal plan, Wright heightened the importance of the simple act of entry.

After one conquers the circuitous path by which Wright made an adventure out of arriving at his houses, "a warm shake of the hand" awaits. The door is simple, wide, and hospitable—"indicative of character and broad ease within, stripped of affectation. No varnish there nor much elaborate 'hardware,'" he instructed as early as 1896.

Inside, he continued, "an atmosphere of quiet strength and well-ordered repose envelops us, refreshes us, and gives us confidence in the personality of the 'owner,' assures us of depth, warmth, and simplicity. The hall, as we look about it, gives us a thrill of welcome...." Even as the more formal Prairie houses evolved into casual Usonians reflecting changing lifestyles, Wright continued to carve out an entry to mark the transition from the outside. In some houses, no more than a half wall, or a planter, or carefully arranged furnishings set it apart.

Snugly low in greeting, the entry ceiling typically bursts the bounds of its compressed height a few steps in, over the living area. "This change in height from the entry to the living room gives a release and lift to the spirit," notes Wright's grandson Eric Lloyd Wright in *Details of Frank Lloyd Wright*. "Usually the entry is placed so that you have only a glimpse of the living room as you enter the residence through the front door. The view is just enough to tantalize and entice you to move into the main room to discover the mystery around the corner."

Techniques Wright used in his entrance halls to compress and release space worked well elsewhere to make houses seem larger and simply more interesting. He varied the levels of ceilings and to a lesser extent of floors to keep spaces fluid and mysterious. In comparison with a low entrance hall or bedroom hallway, a raised living room ceiling seems that much higher, whether it is flat or open to the rafter tops.

Wright's play with levels was one of the ways he manipulated the contrasts at the heart of his architecture: horizontal and vertical, dark and light, solids and voids, open and closed, public and private. He regarded his rooms as open tents, but they had to satisfy the human longing for protective retreats. By offering different levels inside a house, he gave his homeowners both caves and tents from which to choose.

VARIED LEVELS

Compress space in one area, open it in another

In Laura Gale's 1909 house not far from Wright's own in Oak Park, a platform holds the dining room as if on a platter. Set apart just two steps up from the living room, the airy space seems a world unto itself. Both rooms share the same ceiling level, but the compacted dining space makes a cozier, more intimate location for family gatherings around the table. Wright viewed dining as "a great artistic opportunity," one he executed here with great skill.

How high should a ceiling be? In 1945 Wright and Dorothy Parker came to verbal blows on the topic, he taking the side of "democratically" low ceilings based on the size of human inhabitants. "Just for fun let's say the sky *is* the limit," he suggested. "But how many of us could stay out there beneath it if we wanted to?" Admitting that most people want a ceiling as high as possible, Wright went on: "High ceilings pull the walls in. Low ceilings push them away. *There is seldom money for both space and height.*" The architect from the prairie opted for the horizontal line while exploiting the tensions inherent in the contrasts between earth and sky, floor and ceiling.

Wright strove to make his ceilings as comforting as a forest canopy sheltering the ground below. In his Prairie houses he began extending ceilings onto the walls, bringing the plaster down to the windows or a wood band to give "a generous overhead to even small rooms." Continuing the ceiling color to the window tops made the ceiling seem that much taller, and the walls likewise borrowed visual height from the ceiling.

In later designs Wright's ceilings became more like trees growing inside. Wood strips unfolded in cascading planes, leading the eye up to the rafters. Bosky covers of cypress or mahogany brought the outdoors in. Heights fluctuated like swaying branches, low over private areas and higher over public spaces. There Wright was sure to insert a wood deck—a false ceiling—to both interrupt and call attention to the dramatic rise. "The height of a ceiling," he concluded, "should be such that appropriate human scale is maintained in a proportion that makes it unlikely . . . that anyone could guess its 'height' in feet or inches."

CEILINGS
Dramatize heights by fooling the eye

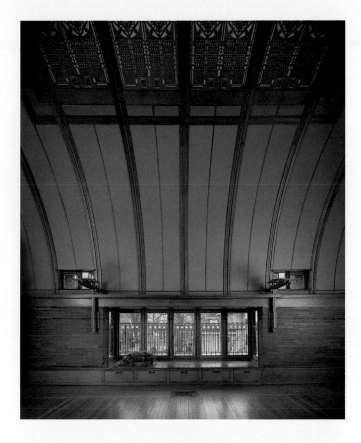

At the Mossberg House (1948) in South Bend, Indiana, the full height of the gabled roof is exploited with a cathedral ceiling over the living room (opposite). Yet Wright moderated this tented "sky" by streaking it with wood and bringing it down to human scale. A shallow false ceiling with built-in lights adds coziness to the intimate seating nook. One of Wright's most dramatic early ceilings covers the playroom in Oak Park built for his children in 1895 (above). Outlined in wood strips mimicking a forest bower, wood-toned plaster swoops down to a low horizontal band below normal ceiling height—thereby aggrandizing its size. The scale here is Lilliputian, given the room's young users.

WALLS AND SCREENS

Reconfigure walls as subtle dividers and screens

**Serving as an architectural sieve—concealing while revealing—
screens and half walls are key tools in visually expanding space.
At the May House (1908) in Grand Rapids, Michigan (opposite, top
left), wood slats screen the entrance and the stairway. A partial
wall in the same house, offering a bouquet of prairie flowers (top
right), marks the dining room without obstructing the traffic
flow. To the left another wall stops short of the ceiling. The interior walls of the Sturges House (1939) outside Los Angeles (bottom left) boldly continue the same brick and redwood used on the
exterior. One of Wright's Usonians, the Smith House (1946) in
Bloomfield Hills, Michigan (bottom right), is enriched with tidewater cypress screens and doors perforated in a stepped motif.**

"The demand for visibility," Wright wrote in 1928, "makes walls
and even posts an intrusion to be got rid of at any cost." By
breaking down confining walls—replacing them with glass outside and natural dividers inside—he made one of his most lasting contributions to how modern houses work. In his hand
walls became not barriers but screens.

At first, with his Prairie houses, Wright treated walls like painted
canvas: "rich, mellow surfaces of color, simply edged, framed and
marked by emphasizing bands of wood." Paintings themselves,
they needed no applied artwork. Light-colored plaster ceilings
merged with the walls, stippled with natural hues and including
perhaps a small frieze or mural but devoid of wallpaper.

Wright also perfected the use of screens and half walls to subtly organize interior space once walls and doors were gone. By
the entrance, along the stairway, or between activity areas,
screens of slatted wood were there and not there. As he por-
trayed them in 1896, "The minute pattern of the wall drops out
at intervals, in twos and threes, becoming naturally a delicate
wood screen...." In his later Usonian houses, wood panels carrying geometric perforations covered windows and clerestories
as well as dividers recalling the delicate shoji screens of Japan.

The most radical change of all was Wright's rediscovery
that—like the log cabins and stone huts of old—walls hewn from
the same materials inside and out achieved the unity of design
he had long sought. Starting with his concrete-block houses of
the 1920s and continuing into the board-and-batten, brick,
block, and stone Usonians, the self-described weaver wove a
seamless fabric with which to naturally clothe the modern home.

By the 1930s, when he began to design his more modest Usonian houses, Wright had long since learned how to insinuate light inside through a house's framework rather than through holes punched in a wall. "You may see that walls are vanishing," he noted with satisfaction in 1954. "The cave for human dwelling purposes is at last disappearing."

After first banding together windows for maximum impact and lowering them for ease of viewing, Wright progressed to using entire walls of windows and doors. What better way to open up a house's private side, secluded away from the street? Glass was his chief weapon in the battle to liberate modern homeowners, increasing the sense of spaciousness inside and expanding horizons outside.

Glass for his floor-to-ceiling window walls was sized in modules to line up with the other building materials, sometimes set into wood mullions continuing the line of the board-and-batten or concrete-block walls. Folding French doors and zigzagged panes make glass seem even less a barrier, reaching out to nature like the casement windows Wright preferred. In the 1940s and 1950s, before anyone knew there was an energy crisis, Wright turned sun catcher with a series of south-facing "solar hemicycle" designs whose elliptical window walls passively capture the sun's rays. Using glass, Wright succeeded in building "broad shelter in the open," inviting nature indoors in all its guises.

WINDOW WALLS

Maximize views and access to the outdoors

Like a glazed smile, the garden room windows of the Laurent House (1949) in Rockford, Illinois (opposite), drink in the sun. The elliptical wall of glass was typical of Wright's solar hemicycle designs. Seemingly interrupted only by the glass walls, the ceiling continues outdoors in the overhang of the roof. The window wall on the private side of the first Jacobs House (1936) in Madison, Wisconsin (above), allows the small house to visually annex space from its yard, which is angled into the ell formed by its two wings.

CLERESTORIES

Place windows high up for privacy, light, and air

Two levels of clerestory windows heighten the drama of the living room in the Brandes House (1952), a late Usonian residence in Issaquah, Washington. In the lower tier, a thin ribbon of glass naturally lights up a secluded sitting area, while a larger clerestory at the ceiling top, underscored with a wood band, runs around the room—an elongated version of the main windows beneath.

Windows, suggested Wright, are like eyes on the face of a house. By this analogy, his clerestories—windows tucked high up into a wall—are expressive eyebrows that add ever-changing character to a room. He used them from the beginning to the end of his career to coax in extra light. These high windows allowed him to hide a multitude of neighboring sins with a wall reaching above eye level yet avoid sacrificing light altogether.

Wright's preference always was to incorporate light right into a structure, rather than use glaring, stand-alone devices. Glass became his favorite light fixture. Especially when filled with art glass in his Prairie years, clerestories sifted geometric patterns onto walls and floors to emulate leaves filtering sunlight through a tree. When filled with less expensive clear glass in the architect's later Usonian houses, these high openings were often mitered to make the corners disappear. Some panels were uninterrupted glass, while others used mullions to mimic the patterns of brick, concrete block, or lower window forms in the rest of the house. Wright's economical Usonians are often distinguished by perforated-wood boards with lively geometric motifs fitted inside and out over fixed or operable panels.

Placed at the natural ceiling line, clerestory windows help make Wright's rooms seem taller and more spacious—adding a surprise, just like a raised eyebrow. They fool the eye in the same way that many of his ceilings do. Not only do clerestories bring in light, they also save on the need for air conditioning by offering cross ventilation up high where heat collects. Using these narrow bands of glass, Wright was able to carefully frame the sky and trees outside as part of a home's interior landscape.

For Wright sunlight equalled freedom, the freedom "of our arboreal ancestors living in trees," as he suggested in 1954. Seeking to reproduce that paradise on earth, he began to incorporate light from above in his own Oak Park home as early as 1895. There he installed a backlighted ceiling grille over the dining table and a similar design beneath a skylight in the upstairs playroom. Lighted artificially or naturally, their carved leaves stencilled patterns below just as sunlight dapples a forest floor. "No glaring fixtures there," Wright noted in 1896, "but light, incorporated into the wall, which sifts from behind its surface opening appropriately in tremulous pattern...."

Wright soon built in "sunlight" and "moonlight," designing natural skylights and electric ceiling fixtures dressed in the nature motifs of his famous stylized art glass. Although that later proved too expensive, he continued to use skylights to usher light into landlocked kitchens, bathrooms, entrances, or wherever light would be uplifting and protect privacy. "The source of light, natural or artificial, was concealed, leaving a slightly mysterious feeling," notes Carla Lind in *Frank Lloyd Wright's Glass Designs.* "It became one of Wright's many illusions."

The magician also made corners disappear with mitered joints of glass. Set at right angles to replace blocky walls of masonry or wood, these invisible panes free up views outside. In Wright's hands glass became a plastic material, seemingly turning corners with ease and emerging directly from other building materials. "Glass and light—two forms of the same thing!" he concluded in 1928.

GLASS FEATURES

Use skylights and mitered corners to add light

At the Jester-Pfeiffer House (1938) in Scottsdale, Arizona (opposite), a round skylight echoes the circular pavilions that form the house, finally built in 1971. Even the headboard continues the spherical shape, intimating the continual presence of the sun. Such natural rifts in the ceiling—windows on the sky—help make "the sky as treasured a feature of daily indoor life as the ground itself," as Wright suggested in 1954. In the 1953 house in Bethesda, Maryland, designed for Wright's son Robert Llewellyn Wright (above), a corner vanishes thanks to a mitered window.

FIREPLACES

Pivot rooms around the family hearth

Made obsolete by mechanical heating systems and increasingly endangered by environmental regulations, fireplaces nonetheless remain a potent symbol of home. The rough stone masonry hearth of Robert and Gloria Berger's 1950 house in San Anselmo, California (above), captures their living room's hexagonal shape. The same materials, gathered by the owners themselves, clad the exterior. Wright also designed a triangular doghouse for the family dog, Eddie. Kenneth and Phyllis Laurent's 1949 house in Rockford, Illinois, has two fireplaces. The one in the living area's "cove," adjacent to the dining nook and the kitchen (opposite), mirrors the house's square grid in lines as straight as its rows of brick.

For Wright, a fireplace radiated with symbolism: of home, of family, of primordial caves, of the sun captured indoors. Although fireplaces were no longer needed for heating when he began his architectural practice—and had long been surpassed by modern technology at the end of his career—they remained a central focus of all his houses. "It refreshed me," he recalled in 1930, "to see the fire burning deep in the masonry of the house itself."

Like other designers who came of age during the Arts and Crafts movement, Wright sometimes called attention to his early fireplaces by framing them in inglenooks, cozy corners where families were meant to gather in the days before television. Soon the hearth, moved to a key inside wall, became the point around which his living areas pivoted. Sheathed in the house's masonry and presenting a cavelike opening underscoring fire's primitive attraction, Wright's fireplaces were a psychological foil for his wide-open plans.

By the time Wright was building Usonia house by house, he had perfected this link between earth and sky. Even in small houses his fireplaces stretch from floor to ceiling clad in earthy brick, stone, or concrete, often rising asymmetrically to fit snugly into the roofline without expensive trim. Their shapes mirror the house's geometric grid, fully integrating the fireplace into the plan. Occasionally one would piggyback on another to warm both the living area and an adjacent study, and in one compact house three were stacked on different levels to draw from the same chimney. Like trees in a forest, the Usonian fireplaces formed the masonry core of each house. Wright called them "the heart of the whole and of the building itself."

WOOD DECKS

Install broad ledges to make a room look wider

At the 1950 Usonian home of Mary and William Palmer in Ann Arbor, Michigan, a wood deck punctuates the triangular living area. The shelf seems to catch the cascading boards of the red tidewater cypress ceiling, contrasting its great height with a reminder of human scale. Wright urged homeowners to drape their wood decks with grasses and other natural bouquets in addition to objets d'art. So bedecked, the ledges, as *House Beautiful* suggested in November 1955, strike "incidental chords of music."

Wright called them "plastic-ribbons" because they tied together his open living areas, wrapping a room and turning corners with agility. These bands of wood at door or window level—flat profiled at first and then expanded as shelves up to two feet wide—served a number of purposes more important than as roosts for a family's treasures, although that use was not overlooked. Wright's decks unify one space with another, beginning perhaps in the entry, circumnavigating the living room, and traveling on into the dining area. Parallel with the floor, they draw a strong line below the ceiling to bring it down to human scale. By emphasizing the horizontal, they make a space seem wider. In later years Wright used these decks as a vehicle for carrying hidden lighting, gaining mystery by indirection.

We may take plumbing, electric lights, and forced heat for granted, but in 1900 these were awkward new technologies to be fitted into a home as seamlessly as possible. Wright, who considered "everything in the nature of a hanging fixture a weakness and naked radiators an abomination," spent his entire career trying to build mechanical systems into the fabric of his residences. His genius in doing so radically altered the shape of the modern home.

For light, "the beautifier of the building," Wright took his cue from the sun, "the great luminary of all life," as he suggested in 1954. First came proper orientation of a house, followed by integral artificial lighting—"as near daylighting as possible." He liked light from above, as if shone inside by the sun, and diffused to soften it in the interest of tranquillity. Wood decks around a room proved tailor made for hiding light, which could be directed up or down. Recessed ceiling fixtures and skylights provided the same overhead illumination as found in nature. Light imbedded in cutout concrete blocks made walls glow from inside. Table and floor lamps and sconces reflected a house's own geometry.

As for heating, Wright realized that if all rooms could be kept equally warm from an invisible source, space could flow freely in a house; walls and doors would not be needed to contain the heat. His solution was what he called gravity heat—hot-water coils set in a bed of crushed rock and covered with a concrete "floormat." Stained red, waxed, and inscribed with the geometric module of the house, these floors allowed warmth to rise naturally from the earth, feet first. With light brought in from above and heat from below, Wright created his own climate.

LIGHTING AND HEATING

Use indirect systems to diffuse light and heat

Calling shadows the architect's brushwork, Wright painted the ceiling of the Palmer House with points of light hidden in the wood deck. The red concrete floor, marked with the house's triangular plan, hides the gravity heating system. This was inspired by a "Korean room" Wright visited in Japan in 1914. The perforated brick wall shielding the kitchen adds another light source.

KITCHENS

Keep the workspace compact and within reach

The kitchen of the Stromquist House (1958) in Bountiful, Utah, is typical for a Usonian. The cutout screen opens only onto the entry, but the tall workspace gains light and air from above. Concrete and wood seamlessly continue the house's primary materials, and cabinets and countertops are all within quick reach. The workspace may have been too compact for some, lacking in windows, and still a woman's preserve, but at least the homemaker was no longer exiled from the rest of the family while she cooked.

When Wright was designing for the families of business executives with servants, he did not have to give much thought to the kitchen. His first examples followed early-twentieth-century standards for food preparation, except perhaps in his appreciation for fine wood and art glass windows. "Make your kitchen fit to live in and have all the little conveniences and necessities well arranged," he suggested in 1894, "for they lessen the petty friction of life that gradually makes things creak and groan." Then he advised: "Get everything on 'ball bearings' where you can." By the time teachers and journalists became his clients, beginning in the mid-1930s, he had to rethink this space.

First Wright renamed it the "workspace," making the kitchen the housewife's efficient "laboratory." And then he took this "kitchen-mechanic" out from behind closed doors and made her "the central figure in her menage"—a hostess entertaining her guests or family. The kitchen was moved away from outside walls, freeing them for family activities, and placed in a central masonry core adjacent to other utilities such as the bathroom and the mechanical systems. To expedite service and cleanup, it was close to the dining alcove although discreetly out of view.

Finished in the same materials as the living areas, Usonian kitchens blend in. Most have limited or no outside views but instead rise high to catch light from a skylight or a clerestory that doubles as a natural exhaust for smoke and cooking odors. Despite their small size—not much larger than a ship's galley—these workspaces brought a sea change for the chef.

At the turn of the twentieth century, dining remained a conspicuous occasion for consumption. For Wright, it was an "artistic opportunity": in dining rooms he could paint a picture of family togetherness, with members gathered upright in his tall-back chairs to take their meals. For his clients it was a chance to show off their daring in hiring such an up-and-coming architect. Wright responded with orchestrated compositions of table and chairs that served as a room within the larger room, reinforcing on a smaller scale the forms, materials, and colors of the larger room and the house itself.

With space at a premium in his smaller Usonians, Wright did what he had long urged to meet the goal of having "as few rooms as necessary," moving diners to an alcove carved out of the main living area. What might have been unthinkable to middle-class homeowners in 1900 became acceptable during the depression years of the 1930s and commonplace by the 1950s, as lifestyles changed and women entered the workforce.

Often located at the junction of the house's wings, the dining nook is convenient to the kitchen. Its table might be an extension of the wall, on which shelves holding the china make their own ornament. Simple chairs of plywood were typically part of the plan. Clever Usonian hosts and hostesses turned to buffets when sit-down dinners would produce more guests than there were chairs. But by borrowing visual space from the larger living area, Wright's dining alcoves stretch the precious commodity of space as far as possible.

DINING AREAS

Set aside part of the living room for dining

As early as 1896, Wright called for a dining area to be "a bright, cozy, cheerful place you involuntarily enter with a smile, not larger than the necessities of this family and current guests require, perhaps a sunny alcove of the living room." By 1939, when the Rosenbaum House in Florence, Alabama, was designed, he got his space-saving dining alcove. The table projects from the board-and-batten wall as if it were another board; shelves and storage above similarly slip into the rhythm of the wall. The owners' Eames chairs fit into the Wrightian aesthetic. Overhead, soft "moonlight" sifts leafy patterns from a perforated ceiling fixture.

When Wright was beginning his practice, bungalows came with built-in furniture—Arts and Crafts proponents recommended it as a means of simplifying and sanitizing the home. Wright took this idea and honed it to perfection, seeing built-ins as a way to unify his interiors and make each a work of art. Attached to the walls as part of the architecture, built-ins would provide "complete harmony, nothing to arrange, nothing to disturb: room and furniture an 'entity,'" as he foresaw in 1896. No less important was that owners would be prevented from moving in too many furnishings that clashed with Wright's vision.

In a small house built-ins save space while they unify interior materials, making rooms look coordinated. Bookcases and buffets become one with the walls; attached sofas clear space in the middle of a room, making it look wider; shelves serve as inconspicuous room dividers; a cantilevered dining table makes a reduced-size dining nook work. Wood decks running around a room do double duty as display and conduits for hidden lighting.

Initiated with Wright's first house (his own in Oak Park) and refined in the Prairie years, built-ins came to play a significant role in the low-cost Usonians, where even the heating was built into the floor. Both the same wood, such as a cypress plywood, and the same module as the rest of the house were used to achieve design unity. Carpenters on site constructed built-ins along with the house itself, but some owners became "fingers on Wright's hands" by turning this into a do-it-yourself project.

BUILT-INS
Build in furnishings to unify and free up space

Typical built-ins include an upholstered sofa at Wright's own home (1889–95) in Oak Park (opposite, top left); beds, dressers, and a desk at the Laurent House (1950) in Rockford, Illinois (top right); bookcases and a bench at the Tomek House (1907) in Riverside, Illinois (bottom left); and at the May House (1908) in Grand Rapids, Michigan (bottom right), a buffet as well as built-in lamps making the dining room table a room within a room.

FURNISHINGS

Make furnishings part of the entire composition

Ann and Eric Brown's 1949 house in Kalamazoo, Michigan, has the modular furnishings Wright liked to design for his Usonians. The mahogany side chairs, end tables, and footstools all can be rearranged as necessary, including for concerts in their living room. For Ann Brown, an artist, shelves were built into the wall opposite the kitchen to permit a changing show of work. The concrete-block hearth seems to float in its glassy pool of water.

With all its built-ins, a Wrightian house seemed almost fully furnished. Yet chairs, tables, lamps, tables with lamps, sofas, plant stands, music stands, Japanese print stands, night stands, beds, desks, windows, carpets, and vases all remained to be created as intrinsic building blocks of each house—little sentinels of the architecture itself. "It is quite impossible," said Wright in 1910, "to consider the building one thing and its furnishings another...."

Heavy Victorian furniture, with its dark plush fabrics and elaborate wood treatments, was totally unsuitable for the rectilinear lines and natural aesthetic of Wright's buildings. Unlike other Arts and Crafts designers, who relished handcraftsmanship, he championed the machine for the architectonic lines it could efficiently manufacture. In the Prairie years, Wright's associates helped him produce his signature chairs with tall, square spindled or slanted backs, art glass and matching lamps, copper vases, fireplace andirons, table linens, sculpture, and anything else needed to make a house a home. As one observer noted in the June 1906 *House Beautiful:* "Simplicity is attained by an avoidance of curves, carvings and meaningless ornaments, and by limiting the pieces of furniture to the actual needs of the occupants, instead of crowding the room with them."

Usonian interiors were even further pared down, with at least half the furnishings built in to conserve the limited space. The other items "at large"—mainly simple plywood chairs, footstools, and tables—were designed to be built on site, sometimes by the owners. Fashioned into rectangles, triangles, hexagons, or circles matching the house's own module and easily moved from place to place, their uses unfold like finely articulated origami.

"Go to the woods and fields for color schemes," Wright advised in 1908. For his buildings the warm, "optimistic" tones found in the earth, the greens of a forest, and the golds and reds of autumn leaves were far more appropriate, he said, than the "pessimistic" blues, purples, pinks, and cold greens and grays to be found at the ribbon counter at Marshall Field's. The Cherokee red of barns dotting the Wisconsin countryside became his signature color, chosen to conjure up the ruddiness of the earth. Occasionally gilt tones would make their way onto the walls or into the fireplace mortar to recall painted Japanese screens.

The architect's palette began with his materials, which he used both outside and in for perfect harmony. Each one—whether wood or brick, stone or concrete, plaster or glass—was treated according to its own nature, never mistreated. Wright suggested that wood, for example, should be left alone, not carved, and only stained to bring out its grain when used in a wall or a table. Plaster might be mixed with sand to underscore its natural origins and painted ("scumbled") with textured colors to simulate natural aging. Underfoot, waxed floor boards recalled the forest floor and waxed red concrete an earthy clay.

Coarse weaves and nubby textiles were used for upholstery as well as for drapery. He insisted that oriental rugs scribe rectilinear lines and area carpets be cut to reinforce a house's geometric module. Not for Wright the "efflorescence of hangings, apoplectic roses bulging from the walls, pears, melons, and grape clusters on tapestry chair seats and miles on miles of nervously overwrought window millinery competing with hysterical portières," as he described the antithesis of his work in 1896.

NATURAL COLORS
Echo nature in the interior design palette

The area surrounding the inglenook of Wright's Oak Park home (1889–95) conjures up visions of a prairie forest. The brick of the fireplace and the oak of the overmantel, with its Arts and Crafts inscription, set a warm, natural tone. Framed with wood bands like a painting, the lower walls evoke a spring bower just leafing out. The same green reappears in the restrained portières and the cushions, while the reading chair adds a touch of fall. Encased in gold, one of Wright's Japanese prints is an ode to simplicity.

ORNAMENT

Integrate decoration into the architecture

When it came to ornament, Wright was squarely in the middle: opposed to the excesses of his Victorian predecessors and equally opposed to the minimalism of his Bauhaus contemporaries. A building without ornament was to him like a face without features. All he demanded was that decoration be integral, "wrought in the warp and woof of the structure," as he wrote in his 1932 autobiography.

Rather than a means to conceal structure, ornament in his hands became a way to make structure more expressive. He

Ornament is obvious in the art glass designed during Wright's Prairie period. This window in the May House (1908) in Grand Rapids, Michigan (above), abstracts stalks of wheat that grow on the prairie. Wright later claimed that concrete was just waiting for the impress of imagination. At the Freeman House (1923) in Los Angeles (right), an ornamental motif unique to the house is stamped into the walls; beside them, perforated blocks with glass serve as light screens. Even the plain glass mirrors the block segments.

parted walls with shimmering panels of art glass, pressed motifs into concrete blocks, outlined ceilings with wood strips, ran decks high around a room, perforated patterns into window screens, angled fireplaces into a jagged roofline, sifted light over a dining table, marked floors with geometric patterns, and contrasted textures from dark to light, rough to smooth. Ornament arose from the way wood was laid for walls or brick was pierced, from the rich color of tinted stucco or grained wood that replaced pictures hung on the wall.

All of Wright's architectural ornament was abstracted— what he called "conventionalization," as seen in the Japanese woodblock prints he collected. Far removed from realism and the three-dimensionality of upholstered flowers, such motifs were designed to stay flat and become a quiet background. Murals avoided competition with their walls, just as rugs emphasized the floor's horizontality. Wright loved the challenge, confessing that ornament "is the most fascinating phase of the work, involving the true poetry of conception."

HARMONY

Relate design motifs to the overall theme

At the May House (1908) in Grand Rapids, Michigan, art glass windows and skylights stencil abstract plant forms onto the carpet, where similar motifs have already been woven in. The table runner picks up the theme with feathery chevrons. Square portholes lining the living room's window wall reappear to border the glass. Both chairs and walls wear the same autumn shade of pumpkin.

Like every note in a piece of music, every feature in a Wright house contributes to the harmony of the composition. From one theme—one basic idea—came all the minor elements of design. In one form or another, that theme was nature.

Wright's interior motifs grew organically from the building. Motifs embroidered on a table runner reinterpret a design used on the carpet, which reinforces patterns in the windows and doors. Although always abstract, his motifs became more so over the years. Stylized flowers pressed into art glass gave way to tabletops cantilevered to match the roofline and then to circles swirling around a carpet or perforations in a wood screen recalling the geometry of the house plan. Producing an order as harmonious as nature's, each contribution furthers a sense of repose and makes the whole greater than the sum of its parts.

Near the turn of the twentieth century, Wright began to rail against homes that were "mere notion stores, bazaars, or junk shops." He countered in 1894 that a home should instead have "one good thing, one really fine thing, be it useful beauty or beautiful use, than wagonloads of the merely rich." Once he made his first trip to Japan in 1905, he found that the Japanese were already practicing his vision of simplicity. Like their woodblock prints, everything unnecessary and insignificant had been eliminated from their homes.

To Wright simplicity meant not the plainness of the side of a barn but a sense of repose, a feeling of completeness, quiet satisfaction in a welcoming home—"qualities that measure the true value of a work of art." By using nature's forms and colors, striving for a coherent theme, maintaining human scale, and integrating furnishings and ornament into a unified composition, a home would offer large rewards regardless of its size. "Only as a feature or any part becomes an harmonious element in the harmonious whole does it arrive at the estate of simplicity," suggested Wright in a 1931 lecture.

When he began to design his small, low-cost Usonians in the mid-1930s, Wright realized that not only the architecture had to change: so did the residents. Some features had to be given up—a separate dining room perhaps, or multiple bathrooms, a kitchen window, a garage—in return for gaining a house with character, one that "stands a good chance of growing more valuable as it grows older."

SIMPLICITY

Simplify the home to simplify life within it

A simple, quiet aura pervades Wright's own bedroom and study at Taliesin (1911–59) in Spring Green, Wisconsin, where he returned in the springtime. Table lamps he designed diffuse light like Japanese shoji screens. Dried autumn leaves bring nature inside. Oriental rugs are lined up in rectilinear patterns. Said Wright in 1894: "It is the duty of every man to raise the character and tone of his own home ... to the highest point his capabilities permit."

WRIGHT-SIZED HOUSES

HOMAGE TO THE SQUARE

The Stockman House

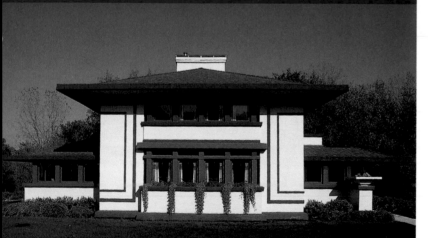

The low hipped roof steps down on either side to smaller replicas over the veranda and the entrance pavilion that cantilever five feet and eight and one-half feet, respectively (above and opposite). Wood bands add a vertical counterpoint while anchoring the stucco, and ribbons of windows flood the house with light. Vines cascading from planter boxes reinforce the relationship between indoors and out. The broad central chimney hints at warmth inside.

At the turn of the twentieth century the *Ladies' Home Journal* was one of a number of home magazines that encouraged new ways of thinking about what a middle-class house should be. Wright obliged by submitting three of his own ideas beginning in 1901. The third, a proposal for "A Fireproof House for $5,000," appeared in April 1907. Essentially a cube that might be confused with the American foursquare houses then in vogue, the two-story residence was designed so that each side of the square could be formed economically of cast concrete using the same wooden forms. Wright was fascinated by concrete, having recently used it for Unity Temple (1904) in Oak Park, Illinois.

Magazine readers were invited to order plans of the house for themselves, and some of them altered Wright's concept to suit their needs. The architect himself adapted his own design that year, using less controversial stucco over a wood frame for the Hunt House (1907) in LaGrange, Illinois. The plan reappeared the next year, reversed, in the home of Dr. George Stockman and his wife, Eleanor, in Mason City, Iowa.

Wright's presence in Mason City (hometown of the *Music Man's* Meredith Willson) to begin work on the City National Bank and Park Inn (1909) caught the Stockmans' attention. Arts and Crafts devotées, they asked him to design a house for them. The Stockman House remained Wright's only completed residence here, for once he and his lover, Mamah Borthwick Cheney, abruptly left for Europe in 1909, the architect fell from grace in "River City." The chance to design the residential enclave of eight houses that became Rock Crest–Rock Glen, one of the country's most cohesive Prairie-style communities, was

awarded in 1912 not to Wright but to Walter Burley Griffin (1876–1937), who had been a trusted associate in Wright's Oak Park studio. With Wright's work leading the way, these buildings soon put Mason City on the architectural map.

In outward appearance, the Stockmans' banded stucco house has much in common with Wright's Prairie masterpieces such as the Willits House (1902) in the Chicago suburb of Highland Park. For his less well endowed clients, he shrunk the features and the plan but retained core qualities from horizontality to integral ornament and openness. Although the Stockman House at first glance appears stolidly square, Wright actually broke out of the box here with a veranda to the left and a sheltered entrance to the right. Both help marry the house to the prairie earth, as he liked. Most important, they free up the center of the house—3,000 square feet including the veranda—for the business of living. The entry and stairs are moved away from the heart of the house, where they would only slice up the space into small rooms. The veranda, by being off to the side, remains a private retreat; no visitors have to cross it to enter, as they would a front porch.

Up the short flight of entrance stairs is a living area that feels as open as any Wright house twice its size. The living room runs the full length of the facade, pulling in light from the prominent band of windows. It borrows visual space from the dining room, which is just partially screened behind the broad brick fireplace. French doors opening to the veranda beyond naturally incorporate that space into the living area as well. In the fourth corner is the slightly offset kitchen

No walls shut off the dining room, which flows easily into the living room with only the brick fireplace to intervene (opposite). A wide slash of mantel marks the horizontal line, which is repeated in the white mortar between the brick courses. An oak deck leads the eye from room to room, echoing the exterior banding. Both the living and dining rooms visually annex the veranda (above).

Wright did not design furnishings for this economical house as he did for many of his commissions. Period photographs document that simple oak Arts and Crafts pieces and items by Gustav Stickley suited its square lines. For the house's museum interpretation as a Prairie-style residence, reproductions have replaced original items long since removed from the rooms. Bedrooms include textiles in coarse weaves with nature motifs. All four benefit from the generous allotment of windows on each side of the symmetrical house, and one bedroom includes a balcony.

alongside its own entrance, plus stairs to the four bedrooms and one bathroom upstairs.

The square plan of this house was one Wright would return to in his quest for compact, economical living spaces during his Prairie period. Four two-story houses in the Ravine Bluffs development (1915) in Glencoe, Illinois, for example, were also based on the "Fireproof" scheme. One-story versions for the prefabricated American System-Built Homes of 1915–17 fit two bedrooms, a bathroom, and the living areas on one floor by converting the dining room into a dining alcove; these plans shared a coziness with ones used for tens of thousands of bungalows then sprouting up coast to coast.

The Stockmans sold their home in 1917, but it remained in residential use until 1987. Faced with threatened demolition for a church parking lot, the house was moved out of harm's way in 1989 by the city with the aid of a private donation. Soon afterward the River City Society for Historic Preservation acquired the Stockman House and has since meticulously restored it as a house museum. On its new site, it sits across the street from the Rock Glen–Rock Crest National Historic District—uniting Wright with the Prairie School he did so much to foster.

"In the attention to detail Wright lavished on this moderately inexpensive house, we can gauge a measure of the significance he attached to this part of his body of work," notes Robert McCoy, a leader of local preservation efforts. "In this beautiful little cameo of his Prairie School design principles, we can come to an understanding of the whole oeuvre of his Prairie School period, the period of creativity called Wright's 'First Golden Age.'"

FEATURES

The cantilevered veranda on one side and the entrance on the other provide balance while extending the house into the landscape.

The low hipped roofs reach out with broad overhangs to maintain the horizontal line.

Exterior and interior wood banding emphasizes "the line of domesticity."

Windows are grouped for more visual impact outside and better views inside.

A wide central chimney telegraphs the hearth around which the house pivots.

The entrance is secluded on the side, adding a sense of mystery while simplifying the facade.

Sequestering the entry in its own pavilion frees up more interior space.

Stairs rise from the entry into the living room, heightening the sense of arrival.

Only a fireplace divides the living and dining areas, giving the illusion of more room.

Built-in bookcases and a dining room sideboard conserve space.

SECOND FLOOR

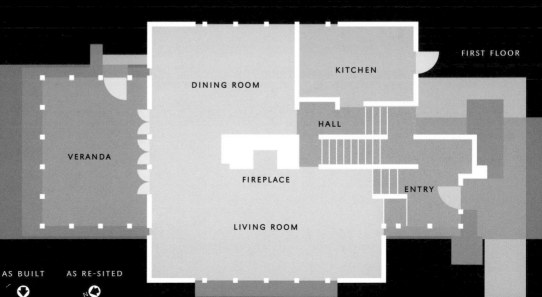

FIRST FLOOR

.09 INCH = 1 FOOT   AS BUILT   AS RE-SITED

> "On a scale such as the Coonley house, flowing spaciousness is relatively easy to achieve because of the size and breadth of the overall building. Here we see the same richness and variety of interior space made possible in more moderate circumstances."
>
> **Bruce Brooks Pfeiffer**
> *Frank Lloyd Wright Monograph, 1907–1913,* 1987

TALL STORY

The Isabel Roberts House

About 1926 a brick veneer was added to cover the original wood-trimmed gray stucco—the first of a number of changes that refined the Roberts House over the years. Although it is majestic enough during the daytime, evening lighting clarifies the spaces (opposite top and bottom). Ongoing research into the garden (above) has uncovered elements such as rock features that point to the work of the noted prairie landscape architect Jens Jensen.

With the first of the Wright house plans commissioned by the *Ladies' Home Journal*—"A House in a Prairie Town," published in February 1901—Wright wrote, "In a house of this character the upper reach and gallery of the central living room is decidedly a luxury." Within seven years he had found a way to afford the luxury of a two-story living room in a house of modest cost. That house was built in 1908 in River Forest, Illinois, for Isabel Roberts, the office manager of his studio in neighboring Oak Park.

Like the innovative Willits House (1901), this Prairie-style residence is one of Wright's cruciform designs—cross shaped in both plan and elevation—just on a smaller scale. The square was banished in favor of projecting shapes that express the nature of the space inside. Similar houses were spun off the same design around the same time, including the Davidson House (1908) in Buffalo, New York, and the Baker House (1909) in nearby Wilmette, Illinois. Wright's attempt to interest Joshua Melson of Mason City, Iowa, in another version for his lot in Rock Crest–Rock Glen was met with rejection (Walter Burley Griffin later built him a magnificent riverside castle instead).

The Roberts House is widely considered one of Wright's stellar Prairie houses. This bookkeeper's residence holds its own against homes of businessmen who usually employ bookkeepers. Roberts began working for Wright in 1903 and, using her art training, is even thought to have assisted with some of the detail drawings of her own home. Although the building permit was issued in the name of her mother, who lived here for a time with her two daughters, Wright's design was clearly meant for an esteemed employee who was rumored to be more than

Intimate and open areas mesh throughout the Roberts House. Space above the living room fireplace is tamped down by the mezzanine, but it soars to the ceiling to release the heart of the room (left and above). This sculpting of space, while not unusual now, was revolutionary in Wright's day. The sectional sofa and ottomans were designed for the house during his renovation in 1955. Windows in the two-story living room, which measures about fifteen by twenty-five feet, overlooked a forest preserve.

that. She moved away about 1916, relocating to Orlando, Florida, where she managed an architectural practice until 1945.

Sequestered behind a wing wall shielding the dining room, the entrance is hidden in the Wright style. Once inside the view extends some seventy feet along the arms of the cross, left toward the glassed-in vitrine for dining and right through the living room and on to the far wall of the garden room. A few steps in, the back wall parts for a golden brick fireplace around which the entire house pivots like a centrifugal force. The living room at the heart of the plan, rising two stories to a pitched ceiling, bursts with light and a sense of freedom that must have been startling in 1908. A mezzanine continues the line of the fireplace up into the quiet zone, where one of the three bedrooms uses this central chimney to carve out its own fireplace. A hall leads to the back of the cross, which also holds the balconied master bedroom, a smaller room, and two bathrooms. In the above-ground basement are a bedroom-study, a bathroom, and utilities.

The interweaving of spaces—one level flowing into two, downstairs floating upward, front meeting back, side linking side—creates a masterfully subtle abstract composition. As Peter Blake assessed it in *The Master Builders,* "Wright had at last broken completely with symmetry and substituted for it a dynamic asymmetry, a balance-in-motion infinitely more complex and infinitely more poetic than the formal disciplines of

Diners can see from the dining room to the far side of the house, where the garden room (above) was enclosed for year-round use. Its star attraction is an English elm lovingly built in by Wright and pampered in later renovations. Although the budget did not allow elaborate glass, diamond-pane windows used in the living room and repeated in the dining room (opposite) create a distinctive lattice-work theme. More light shines down from a perforated-wood fixture above the table, a 1950s Wright design for Heritage-Henredon.

Bedrooms are secluded in the rear of the cross-shaped plan, buffered by a spacious mezzanine (top) reached by discreet stairs across from the entry. Built-in storage adds to the usefulness of this space, where not a static corner can be found. The master bedroom (above), made from two smaller bedrooms in 1955, has both a balcony and a garden view. The same diamond-pane windows seen downstairs reappear here, unifying the house's design.

past civilizations." Difficult enough to do in any size house, Wright succeeded in molding space in a small house to match the spirit of a larger one. "I don't think we really understood, until we moved into this house, the power of a well-configured plan," admitted Carol and William Pollak, recent owners.

Wright was approaching ninety years of age when the fourth owners, Warren and Ruth Terry Scott, were finally able to get him to come back to River Forest to improve the house in 1955. After a piano prelude, he walked with them through the house, as Brendan Gill relates in *Many Masks*, pointing out corners cut in 1908. "I got the impression," Warren Scott recalled, "that he had done the job as cheaply as possible because it was a secret gift to Isabel."

Among many changes made then to reinforce and upgrade the house, he enlarged the entry, added stepped blond Philippine mahogany over the original plaster ceilings and laid Tennessee crab apple flagstone flooring on the main level, made the porch into a garden room by using windows in place of screens, and removed a partition to open the view from the dining room to the garden room. He also added steel beams to the mezzanine and reconfigured it from octagonal to almost rectangular, added built-ins and indirect lighting in the dining room, converted two bedrooms into a master bedroom, doubled the size of the kitchen, and added two bathrooms. Today the Roberts House represents the pinnacle of Wright's Prairie years, overlaid with ideas from the Usonian period. Said Wright in 1955, "The Isabel Roberts house is one of our best houses and I would not like to see anything happen to spoil it."

FEATURES

- Although filling two stories plus a cellar, the house appears from the outside to be a single story high because it stretches wide with wings under a low roof.
- Its cruciform plan, repeated in the exterior elevation, offers an inherent balance if not exact symmetry.
- Different ceiling heights compress and release space, defining different rooms.
- Interlocking spaces are separated not by doors but by changing angles of vision.

- Clerestories tucked under the eaves on the sides allow light to stream in naturally, from above.
- The balconied two-story living room offers a sense of freedom instead of a confining ceiling.
- A tree growing through the garden room roof impishly integrates nature into the design.
- Diamond-pane windows—as Wright used in his first house, his own Oak Park home—are a simple screening treatment appropriate for a modest home.

BASEMENT

LAUNDRY   PANTRY

REAR ENTRY

KITCHEN   HEATING

DINING ROOM   FIREPLACE   GARDEN ROOM

ENTRY

LIVING ROOM

FIRST FLOOR

N   .065 INCH = 1 FOOT

BEDROOM   BEDROOM

HALL   BATH

MAID

BALCONY

MASTER BEDROOM

MEZZANINE

LIVING ROOM BELOW

SECOND FLOOR

"What this country needs is a decent $5,000 house," Katherine and Herbert Jacobs challenged Wright in 1936. "Can you build it?" He came pretty close, bringing in their 1,300-square-foot house in Madison, Wisconsin, for just $5,500, including his fee. Wright had been searching his entire career for a way to house a family in something other than a poor man's version of a mansion. Usonia Number One, as it is sometimes called, radically altered the traditional conception of home. Similar plans predate the Jacobs House, but theirs was the first Usonian to be built, launching the series of 140 Usonian homes that occupied Wright's last quarter century.

Fresh from designing the tour de force of Fallingwater (1935), Wright relished the chance to flesh out his ideas of what architecture suited for a democracy should look like, a goal he had identified in 1910. Testing Herbert Jacobs, a reporter for the *Capital Times,* and his family, which then included young daughter Susan, Wright asked them, "Would you really be interested in a $5,000 house? Most people want a $10,000 house for $5,000." But, in the midst of the Great Depression, there was no doubt that they had to economize. The Jacobses did not yet have a property (Wright later made them trade their first one for a double lot 120 feet wide by 126 feet deep) or a mortgage. A building association manager who liked Wright's work fortuitously stepped in to offer financing when others shied away.

Wright's plan for this new American family was the essence of simplicity: an L shape in one story that turns its back to the street but opens its arms on its private side to embrace a large garden. Living areas occupy one wing, sleeping rooms the

"Simplifications must take place. Mr. and Mrs. Jacobs must themselves see life in somewhat simplified terms. ... We cannot have an organic architecture unless we have an organic society."

Frank Lloyd Wright
The Architectural Forum, January 1938

ARCHITECTURE FOR DEMOCRACY

The First Jacobs House

The living room hides behind a board-and-batten wall on the street side broken only by a row of high clerestory windows (opposite top). At left the carport wall shields the entry. Flat, overhanging roofs diverge at the juncture of the ell, marked by the brick core holding the fireplace, kitchen, and bathroom. On the private side, all is glass, ringed by a terrace leading to the garden (bottom). "Light and shadow were the free building blocks that Wright knew so well and used so freely," noted Herbert Jacobs.

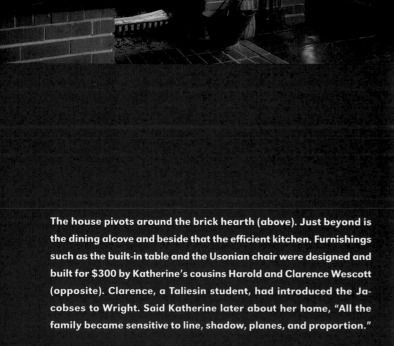

other, all open to nature with floor-to-ceiling walls of windows. Where the two wings come together is a brick anchor: a masonry core containing the chimney, the kitchen, and the bathroom, the latter two located in close proximity to save on plumbing. The kitchen, lighted by high clerestory windows and borrowing views from the living area, vents its cooking odors out the windows. In sight in the crook of the ell is the compact dining nook, the "sunny alcove" of the living room that Wright had been eager to try since 1896. Down a hallway (Wright called them galleries) along the house's side lie two bedrooms, a small shop area, and a study.

"You will have the sense of space—not space itself but the sense of space—which most people pay $10,000 for," Wright alerted the Jacobses. Despite the small dimensions all around, he was right. The living area, thirty by eighteen feet, rises to a generous nine feet, four inches, which makes the bedrooms, at seven feet, three inches high, suitably cozy but in scale with their smaller size. The kitchen tops out at eleven feet, seven inches to compensate for its eight-by-seven-foot area, a little over half of it given to floor space. Natural light, extensive storage, and the ability to see the rest of the family made it a well-appointed laboratory in which Katherine Jacobs prepared buffets for forty members of the Taliesin Fellowship. One space borrows views from another, just as the inside borrows views of the outdoors from the house's thirty-seven windows. Twenty-five doors, well over the standard two, placed nature at the family's feet.

Equally efficient were the materials and the way they were put together to stay within the Jacobses' budget, which Wright for

The house pivots around the brick hearth (above). Just beyond is the dining alcove and beside that the efficient kitchen. Furnishings such as the built-in table and the Usonian chair were designed and built for $300 by Katherine's cousins Harold and Clarence Wescott (opposite). Clarence, a Taliesin student, had introduced the Jacobses to Wright. Said Katherine later about her home, "All the family became sensitive to line, shadow, planes, and proportion."

FEATURES

- Materials are economically limited to wood, brick, cement, insulating paper, and glass.
- Walls are built of a uniform "sandwich" of wood, insulation paper, and plywood as well as of brick, unifying inside and out.
- The flat roof was less expensive to build.
- Coils for steam (later hot water) embedded in a concrete slab permit heat to rise naturally from the floor.
- Gravity heating allows an open plan without the need for walls to contain heat.
- Wood used as the interior finish eliminates labor-intensive paint, plaster, wallboard, and wallpaper.

- In contrast to the public side along the street, the private side embraces the outdoors with window walls facing a garden.
- The dining room has been superseded by a simple dining alcove carved out of the living area and opened up with windows.
- The kitchen is compact, practical, vented outside, and open to the rest of the house while freeing the house's perimeter walls for the living spaces.
- A central core combines utilities in one place.
- A cantilevered carport replaces a more expensive garage.

STUDY

SHOP

MASTER BEDROOM

GALLERY

BEDROOM

TERRACE

DINING ALCOVE

BATH

KITCHEN

FIREPLACE

LIVING ROOM

ENTRY

CARPORT

N

.09 INCH = 1 FOOT

the first and only time guaranteed by contract to meet. To simplify the building process and make use of standardized materials, he developed a grid, part of his unit system, of two by four feet across (inscribed on the floor) and thirteen inches high. He limited his construction palette to wood, brick, concrete, insulating paper, and glass. He used a concrete slab in lieu of a foundation, placing the heating coils in it on a bed of sand to warm the house naturally, from the earth. He "took the factory to the house" with "sandwich" walls serving outside and in. He used low-cost pine boards, paying for redwood battens himself to get the contrast he wanted. He snagged rejected bricks and glass. He flattened the tar and gravel roof, eliminating gutters and downspouts. He parked the car in a simple carport instead of a garage.

But most of all Wright taught this pioneer family how to simplify their lives along with the architecture. They did some construction work themselves, enlisted family to create their furnishings, grew their own vegetables, and took donations from eager sightseers to pay the architect's fee. "The Jacobses were willing to have their house serve as a laboratory," suggests Brendan Gill in *Many Masks.* "They were also willing to serve as guinea pigs in that laboratory." Feeling the city encroaching, they decided in 1942 to move farther out to the countryside. There the Jacobs family embarked all over again on an architectural adventure with Wright, waiting six years for their equally groundbreaking solar hemicycle house. "The sense of living 'wedded to the ground and in harmony with the seasons' is a great gift of Wright to his clients," concluded Herbert Jacobs after twenty years of living in Wright's new world of Usonia.

Bookcases were fitted into the grid system both to organize belongings and to stiffen the walls. Given its experimental nature, the house was in need of attention by the 1980s. John Eifler, a restoration architect, was called in to repair the roof, the concrete slab holding the gravity heating, the twelve-foot carport cantilever, and windows and doors. Insulation and thermal windows were added, and a dark exterior stain was sanded back to the original color.

> "After having experienced it [a Wright house], no one could ever go back to the painted box, which is all the ordinary house really is, however elaborate. . . . It is the only kind that has anything to offer the spirit."
>
> Loren Pope, "The Love Affair of a Man and His House"
> *House Beautiful,* August 1948

LOREN'S LOVE AFFAIR

The Pope-Leighey House

Plain cypress boards take a flight of fancy just below the roof and down the living room side, where perforated cutouts shower the house simultaneously with light and built-in pattern (above and opposite). The end with the children's room is marked by shutters in a more elaborate design. Cantilevered roofs add a sense of majesty to the 1,200-square-foot Usonian, which is now open to the public.

What struggling young journalist today would even think of approaching the country's leading architect and pleading, "Will you create a house for us? Will you?" But in 1939 Loren Pope, an editor at the *Washington Star*, did just that, following in the footsteps of Herbert Jacobs. Pope wrote a long letter to Frank Lloyd Wright and—ever the optimist—enclosed a site map of his acre and a half lot in suburban Virginia that detailed its contours and trees. Pope had discovered Wright's architectural ideas in a *Time* article and then borrowed and quickly bought his own copy of the architect's 1932 autobiography. "From *An Autobiography* on," Pope later recalled, "my bride and I stopped buying Colonial reproductions or thinking about the picket-fenced Cape Cod we were planning to build. Instead, my friends began telling me I was a little giddy to think about approaching the great, expensive, and imperious Frank Lloyd Wright." Because "faith filters out fear and some error," he decided that "the master would listen to someone who wanted one of his works so much."

After reading Wright's life's story, the newspaperman had tracked him down in Washington, extracting from Wright an assertion that he designed houses only for people like Pope "who deserved them." Soon the editor wrote to the person he called "the great creative force of our time": "There are certain things a man wants during life and of life," his letter opened. "Material things and things of the spirit. The writer has one fervent wish that includes both. It is for a house created by you. . . . [O]nly you can create one that will become for us a home."

Within two weeks came the reply from Taliesin: "Of course I am ready to give you a house." So began a year-and-a-half

process that put the Popes and their young son in one of Wright's first Usonian houses in early 1941. Nothing was standard issue: not the construction loan (finally offered by Pope's newspaper), not the contractor (no one would commit to a price for such an out-of-the-ordinary design), not the construction process (a Taliesin apprentice came to Virginia to be Wright's alter ego), and certainly not the design itself.

Expressing admiration for the Jacobs House (1936) in Madison, Wisconsin, Pope gave his new architect a wish list for his home, from winter sun, summer breezes, and "blessed shade" to books ("a lot of them"), plenty of closet space, a study, and a fireplace ("essential, of course"). Charlotte Pope preferred a separate dining room; Loren did not. Above all, they wanted the inside and the outside unified. "When one asks, 'Where does the house begin and the garden end; where does the garden end and the house begin?' even you can't say," suggested Pope, paraphrasing one of Wright's most important precepts. The journalist, working for an income of $3,000 a year, warned the notoriously spendthrift architect that "a $5,500 house is just about our limit." With a redesign to shrink the footprint to 1,200 square feet, with Pope serving as general contractor—and cheerleader—and with the family's close attention to everything from the bricks and boards to

Wright designed the straightforward plywood furniture in the living-dining area (opposite) to be built on site to save time and money. Easily movable to suit changing needs, each piece was intended to reflect the architecture—little offshoots of the overall plan. Here and at the opposite end of the living area (above), the cutout clerestory draws the eye upward to visually raise the ceiling.

piano hinges for the closets, the house was brought in for $7,000, a typical overrun even for Wright's budget-minded clients.

Although the house appears simple, in reality it interweaves spaces like a complex three-dimensional fabric. Hovering over the entry hall is a comforting low ceiling, yet a few feet forward, down a brief flight of stairs, the living area seems to stretch upward with the change in floor level. To the left a dining table nestles in its own space, anchored by a low, lighted ceiling and framed by a brick wall as well as doors leading to the terrace (contrasting solid and void). Diners can steal visual space from the overall living area, including the fireplace nook directly across. Just beyond, more French doors to the porch invite nature inside, blurring the distinction between indoors and outdoors exactly as Loren Pope asked. Built-ins—cabinets with those expensive piano hinges in the entry and shelves for books and china in the living and dining areas—push necessities to the sides to free up room in which to move around. Rather than one long space, the living area is actually a series of skillfully carved-out activity centers. Over it all an ever-changing symphony of light cascades down from the perforated clerestory windows that travel around the room to form the house's leitmotif.

Back up the steps and behind the brick fire wall is the compact kitchen. Its high ceiling and equally slender window, punctuated by a planter box below for herbs, add light if not space. A utility room shares this brick core of the house. Next to it, to the right of the entrance, is the sanctum, an office retreat specified by Pope. Down a narrow hallway lie the bathroom, master bedroom, and children's room.

Tucked into the L-shaped junction of the living and sleeping zones, the dining area (opposite) gains both privacy and a view; the inset terrace serves as an outdoor room, increasing the living space. Lights recessed into the low ceiling overhead eliminate the need for separate fixtures, as do the built-in shelves. As if composing an architectural symphony, Wright returned to the geometric theme of the house's wood cutouts in the children's bedroom (above).

More perforated cutouts placed over clerestory windows add light to the bedroom hallway (top). A window wall on the house's private side lights up the master bedroom (above). Gravity heating coils, since restored, lie beneath the waxed concrete floor.

In August 1948, a year after the Popes moved farther out into the countryside, Pope wrote about his architectural "love affair" in *House Beautiful*. The design is honest, he wrote, "because it is a work of principle . . . and being honest, it is both eloquent and quiet." Marjorie and Robert Leighey eagerly became the next owners. At first Marjorie felt the need for more storage space but then remembered Wright's advice "that possessions merely clutter one's life." She came up with a plan to serve salad from a bowl at the table in order to fit in more dinner guests. She built a garden shed to store tools, not to mention the turkey roaster that had been underfoot in the kitchen. And both cultivated "grace and humor . . . when it was necessary for one to back up, to let the other by in a . . . narrow passage." Simplicity became their watchword. "Simplicity of possessions gradually expands to include simplicity in manner, action, dress, decoration, and interpersonal relationships. Liberation from things releases deeper imaginative, intellectual and creative processes. . . ." For Marjorie Leighey as for the Popes, there was "no point in the house where one feels spatially bound." Even though small, to her it seemed large; it was simple yet complex, proud yet humble—paradoxes that spelled home.

Five months after her husband died in 1963, Marjorie Leighey was notified that a highway was about to take the place of her home. In 1964 she donated it to the National Trust for Historic Preservation, which relocated it at one of its other properties. Recently dismantled again, moved slightly, and rebuilt, the economical house and the Federal-style mansion nearby now show radically different solutions to housing families in style and comfort.

FEATURES

- Deep roof overhangs emphasize the horizontal line, exaggerating the size of the house.
- Primary materials are limited to cypress, brick, and glass.
- Materials are repeated inside and out to achieve architectural unity and simplicity.
- The house's intimate scale is based on the human figure.
- The entrance's dropped ceiling and raised floor level make the living area seem taller by contrast.
- Space flowing around corners breaks up the open plan.

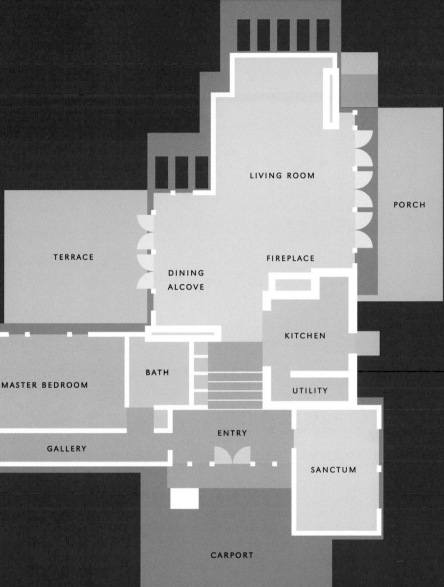

LIVING ROOM

PORCH

TERRACE

FIREPLACE

DINING ALCOVE

KITCHEN

CHILDREN'S ROOM

MASTER BEDROOM

BATH

UTILITY

GALLERY

ENTRY

SANCTUM

CARPORT

AS PLANNED   AS BUILT   AS RE-SITED   .1 INCH = 1 FOOT

- Built-ins free up space in the middle of the rooms, making narrow areas appear wider.
- The living area annexes the terrace as an outdoor room.
- Privacy is preserved by restricting window walls to the side away from the street.
- All ornament, such as the wood cutouts, grows out of the materials themselves.

SMALL WONDER

The Sturges House

The trellised terrace off the living area and bedrooms (opposite, top left) serves as a welcome outdoor room offering expansive vistas. On the exterior, lapped boards and deeply raked brick underscore the house's horizontality even as it pushes up to look out over its neighborhood (top right). Beams in the living room (bottom left), which increase the feeling of height, continue out onto the terrace to form the trellis. "Origami" chairs (bottom right) were designed by Wright. Beyond the dining nook along a short hallway are the kitchen, two bedrooms, a bathroom, and storage.

After seeing the special January 1938 edition of *The Architectural Forum* featuring Wright's work (and guest edited by him), George and Selma Sturges wasted little time in writing to the architect. "We had been thinking vaguely of building a house, when the [magazine] arrived last week," wrote George. "To our great excitement, the house you built for Mr. Jacobs seemed to be exactly the house we want." They also liked its $5,500 price. Having found out from Herbert Jacobs that Wright was planning to design some houses in the Los Angeles area, the couple asked if they could have one for themselves, using the Jacobs House (1936) in Madison, Wisconsin, "as a point of departure."

The Sturgeses had in fact already purchased a double pie-shaped lot in Brentwood Heights whose slope was as steep as the piece of pie was pointed. It was just the type of challenge Wright relished. His response was to give the Sturgeses a point of their own, on which he cantilevered an 870-square-foot design that soars into space like a bird leaving a tree. The tradeoff for the extra expense of building *en pointe* was that the site was spared the excess grading and damage to the natural vegetation that would have come with a more traditional solution.

Perched on its brick pedestal, which holds a workshop installed at the owners' request, the little tree house keeps its own counsel on first approach. Its back is turned to the driveway, and the siding of lapped redwood, originally stained a rust color, gives few hints of welcome. Crossing the threshold from the carport plaza and moving directly into the living area, mystery turns to clarity, darkness to light. The entire southeastern facade, the house's private side, frames a view of the Los Angeles megalopolis

below. Broad glass doors swing out to expand the petite size of the living and sleeping areas onto a wooden terrace that surrounds two sides of the rectangular house. The square module on which the design was built, incised into the red concrete floor, continues overhead in a trellis that filters its square motif onto the wood deck while offering a modicum of needed shade.

Exterior materials come inside, making a seamless transition from outside in. Brick used for the pedestal and chimney is echoed in an over-sized "wall of flame" that allows the small house to think big. Across from it, glass sparkles in contrast. The red concrete floor below stands in for the earth, while the redwood overhead recalls the trees in which the house nestles. A header course of brick on the fireplace segues into built-in wooden shelves defining the cozy dining alcove. All is as precise as a ship's cabin. Earth, air, and fire taken care of, only the fourth element gave the Sturgeses pause. The soft redwood admitted more rainwater than they wanted, leading them to dub their home "Standing Water," the California kin of Wright's famed Fallingwater.

Framed by deeply inset windows bringing light to the kitchen and the bathroom, a stairway leads to a rooftop deck. Sunlight transforms the perforated trellis into a stencil that paints natural patterns on the brick walls and the concrete floor of the forecourt.

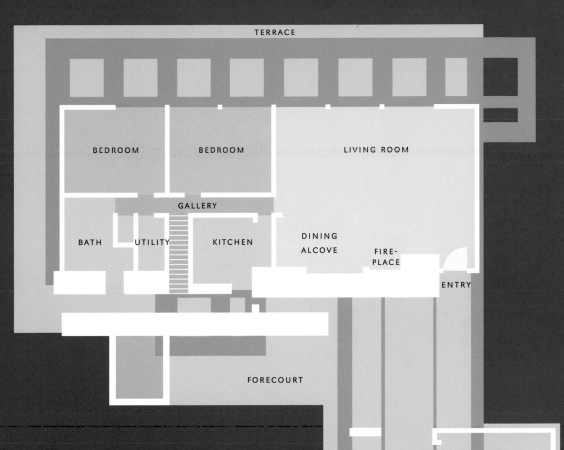

TERRACE

BEDROOM

BEDROOM

LIVING ROOM

GALLERY

BATH

UTILITY

KITCHEN

DINING ALCOVE

FIRE-PLACE

ENTRY

FORECOURT

CARPORT

F E A T U R E S

- Cantilevering the house over the hillside makes the best use of an almost unbuild-able site.
- Terrace walls provide privacy without sac-rificing the view.
- An overhead trellis shades the terrace while repeating the house's geometric module.
- The living area's high ceiling creates a sense of spaciousness.
- Window walls open the interior, including the two bedrooms, to the outdoors.

- In the mild climate of the Los Angeles area, the generous terrace is a true out-door room.
- The dining alcove forms a natural exten-sion of the massive fireplace wall.
- Space for a basement workshop was cre-ated in the brick pier on which the house pivots.
- Tall eucalyptus trees add a vertical coun-terpoint to the horizontality of the house.
- As much drama as possible has been ex-tracted from 870 square feet of living space.

.09 INCH = 1 FOOT

Dr. Isadore Zimmerman, a urologist, and his wife, Lucille, who served as his nurse, lived in a large traditional home in Manchester, New Hampshire, in 1948 but had a "vague, inarticulate feeling that there was much that was wrong with it." Wanting to "avoid adding a new antique to the city's architecture," they purchased a wooded three-quarter-acre lot in the city's north end and proceeded to discard one architect before library research led them to Wright. "It seemed frustrating that he might be beyond our reach," they recalled. "However, we discovered in *House Beautiful* magazine an article by Loren Pope, a client of his, in which he assured the reader that Frank Lloyd Wright was no more expensive than any other architect."

A letter and a visit to Taliesin later, a sketch emerged in fall 1950. Drawings did not come until March 1951. Wright was finally very busy: although he designed fifteen houses in 1949, six of which were built, by 1950 he was at work on thirty-eight; twenty-one of these made it off the drawing board. His postwar clients, like the Zimmermans, tended to have more money and more land. Their higher expectations, coupled with better availability of materials, added more variety to his Usonian palette.

The childless couple gently conveyed a number of requests to their architect. Topping their wish list—which ran to kitchen fixtures, closets, and a place for Lucille to sew—was that their new home accommodate fellow musicians with acoustics good enough to filter sound into every room. The doctor, once a member of the New Hampshire Symphonic Orchestra, was proficient on the violin and piano; Lucille played the piano and cello. Wright, a pianist who viewed architecture as a symphonic

GRACE NOTES

The Zimmerman House

Red brick outlined in white puts the house in New England's Georgian tradition (opposite top). The clerestory of perforated concrete blocks, a favorite Wright material, offers privacy yet directs light into the living area. The roof at right jogs for a window. Walls vanish on the private side to invite light inside (bottom). The lantern atop the projecting master bedroom, seen from the house's storage room and carport end, lights the kitchen (above).

composition, was eminently sympathetic. They probably should not have admitted that they were "willing to make all the necessary financial sacrifices to make this the most comfortable and convenient house for us. . . ." The estimated price tag of $36,000 eventually exceeded $50,000.

With a little more than 1,700 square feet of enclosed space, the Zimmerman House is one of Wright's small miracles. It cost more because of its special features: an all-brick exterior, a clay tile roof, steel framing for the gabled roof, walls and ceilings of clear Georgia cypress, cast-concrete front windows, cast-concrete wall copings and window sills, extensive built-ins and storage, and skilled carpentry for the highly detailed interior. Earlier Usonians typically used board-and-batten walls inside and out, flat roofs of tar and gravel, no copings, and few one-of-a-kind features; some owners even did their own contracting or construction. The first contractor here, unused to Wright's way of thinking, did so much work incorrectly that it had to be redone and he was replaced.

Once the Zimmermans moved into the house in 1952, it was every note of the Usonian sonata they had composed in their own minds. Past the boulder marking the entry, a low hallway

Bands of concrete on the brick fireplace echo the exterior coloring (above). Shelves wrap around the corner, hinting at the dining alcove sequestered beyond. French doors to the terrace enlarge the space. The garden room's brick piers and wall of windows make it look wider, while the low furnishings stretch it higher visually (opposite). In the far corner is the custom music stand. By carrying the plantings through the glass, continuing the floor line through the wall and the roofline through the windows, and extending the ceiling pattern onto the overhang, Wright visually exploded the room's apparent size and its sense of spaciousness.

six feet, seven inches high (an inch taller than usual) unfolds into the house's major space: the eleven-foot-high living room, called the garden room, which stretches out thirty-six feet long. Its seventeen-foot width is a mere formality, given that its full wall of windows and doors annex the great outdoors. At the far end, past the twenty-four-foot-long built-in sofa, an intimate space was carved out for the musical evenings the Zimmermans envisioned. In it they placed the only piece of furniture brought from their previous home, a Steinway grand. And next to it went an octagonal quartet stand and stools like those Wright had designed for himself. Opposite the music corner, an asymmetrical brick fireplace rises to meet the burnished cypress ceiling.

Peeking out from behind the hearth is the built-in dining table, framed by shelves that make an art of the daily china. The kitchen, lighted on high by a clerestory lantern, occupies the masonry core along with the utilities and the two adjacent bathrooms. Beyond, the master bedroom elegantly pushes out the essentially in-line plan into a truncated L shape. A guest room to the left of the entrance conforms to the shape of the land without displacing the roof's taut horizontal line. "To move through the house is to move through a symphony of heights, widths, darkness, and light," observe the restoration architects Tilton + Lewis Associates. "The dark, narrow entrance hall makes the living room seem even higher and lighter—the same with the hall to the master bath and bedroom. Each space gains in intensity by contrast to the transition space preceding it."

As in every Wright house, nature is the leitmotif here. Off the garden room, a terrace coaxes the indoors into the yard. Glass

The kitchen makes up in height what it may lack in floor space (opposite, top left). Taking in the terrace, yard, and living room, the dining alcove feels larger than it is (top right). Built-ins unify the guest room and the rest of the decor while saving space (bottom left). The master bedroom gains height from the gabled roof (bottom right). The cypress board-and-batten ceiling becomes the roof soffit, rendering it difficult to tell where the interior stops (above).

Four garden room windows framed in wood focus the view outside. Beneath them, raised planters inside and out link the house to nature. The red concrete floor underneath holds a gravity heating system that was restored following the Zimmermans' conversion to forced air. An oil boiler sends heated water into the cast-iron pipes—warming the feet first, when it works as Wright intended.

doors and mitered windows blur the distinction between inside and out. Five brick piers shelter raised planter boxes that draw the eye toward their matches outdoors. Above the boxes hang square windows framed like works of art, set into larger glass panes to mirror the small square clerestory windows set in concrete on the opposite wall. Both the red concrete pad inscribed with the house's four-by-four-foot module and the ceiling spill without interruption onto the terrace, expanding the house beyond its drawn boundaries. "We move so freely back and forth between indoors and out that our whole life seems to be spent under the stars and sun," Lucille told readers of the October 1959 *House Beautiful,* a memorial issue on Wright's work.

As much care was taken with the furnishings, which were designed by Wright and made locally. Thirty-six freestanding pieces joined the built-ins, all in cypress. Handmade fabrics from New York in rust and gold linen, woven with Lurex thread, colored the house like autumn leaves. Japanese paper inserts in the lamps, an eighteenth-century Japanese screen, primitive artifacts, pottery, and sculpture lent an antique cast. No paintings were needed. "It doesn't demand ornament as some houses do," noted Lucille.

On the Zimmermans' deaths, "the most beautiful house Mr. Wright ever built," as they called it, was willed to the Currier Gallery of Art, which undertook a top-to-bottom restoration before opening it to the public in 1990. Close by on the same street sits the Kalil House of 1955, a Usonian Automatic whose owners obviously were inspired by the pioneering Zimmermans.

FEATURES

- A long, low roof and a continuous band of concrete-rimmed window openings on the front side emphasize the horizontality of this in-line (rectangular) plan.
- The gabled roof, rare in a Usonian design, has a gentler 1-to-4 pitch on the south, the private side, while the 3-to-5 pitch on the north, the front side, allows a high ceiling.
- The greater roof overhang on the south (private) side provides shade not needed on the north, where the overhang is minimal.
- A large front entrance and low roofline increase the house's apparent size.
- The front clerestory windows fill the entire wall above the sill line.
- Spaces pivot around the asymmetrical brick fireplace, which shields the dining alcove, kitchen, and utility core.

- The high living room ceiling is dramatized by a lower deck that fools the eye, while the low entrance hall makes the living room ceiling feel even higher by contrast.
- Brick columns set at right angles to the windows make the garden room seem wider.
- A glass gable and skylight bring light into the kitchen and master bathroom, located away from exterior windows.
- Built-ins such as the sofa, dining table, and shelves free up interior space.
- The terrace is incorporated as an outdoor room with a ceiling pattern, flooring, and plantings that continue outside through glass doors and windows.

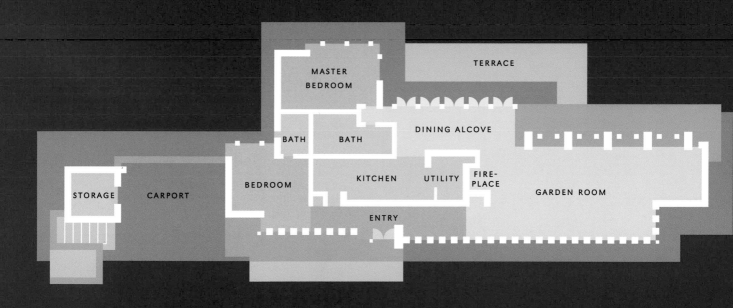

.065 INCH = 1 FOOT

> "Here then, within moderate means for the free man of our democracy, with some intelligence and by his own energy, comes a natural house designed in accordance with the principles of organic architecture.... [I]t yet establishes the democratic ideal of variety—the sovereignty of the individual."
>
> **Frank Lloyd Wright,** *The Natural House,* **1954**

ARIETTA

The Tracy House

Like a red carpet unrolled, the entrance reaches out in a grand gesture belying the house's small size. Steps colored to match the floor inside spill down the gentle incline alongside the low garden wall, which stretches toward the carport. Solid concrete blocks, broken by a double clerestory row, keep the public side private. Wright signed his name in red close to the secluded front door.

At first rebuffed in their desire to have Wright design a house for them, William and Elizabeth Martha Tracy persevered. This self-described "quiet couple (but not dull)" began by asking the architect's secretary, Eugene Masselink, to intercede for them. William, trained as an architect himself, in 1953 was working as an engineer, and Martha had taken art courses at Michigan State from Alma Goetsch and Katherine Winckler, proud owners of their own Usonian house designed by Wright in 1939. The Tracys' lot, on the edge of a cliff overlooking Puget Sound ten miles south of Seattle, was "a sight to behold," William explained, ticking off the flora—fir, madrona, alder, flowering dogwood, shrubs, and ferns—that would bring nature to their doorstep. "Many people saw Wright as a designer of buildings. We saw him as more than that," he recalls. "To us he was a symbol of the American ideals of Washington and Jefferson."

But William Tracy's suggestion of a cantilevered masterpiece, perhaps one resembling the Sturges House (1939) in Los Angeles, went nowhere. Citing the Tracys' small budget, Wright begged off. The couple then approached Milton Stricker, a former Taliesin apprentice. Sensing how much they wanted Wright to create a home for them, he agreed to give up the commission and try instead to twist Wright's arm just a little. It worked, nudged along by the couple's offer to accept one of the architect's "patented block construction used with red cedar or redwood."

This was a reference to Wright's Usonian Automatic system, developed in 1949 as a way to make his 1920s California "textile-block" houses affordable. Implying assembly-line construction

on site, his name for these new concrete-block houses indicated that the work would be so simple that the houses would practically build themselves—with a little help from the homeowners. Instead of patterned blocks as in the earlier designs, the Usonian Automatics used coffered blocks that could be juggled in any number of ways to imprint each house with its own individuality. Blocks were used for the roof as well as walls inside and out, either in single or double layers; the latter had an insulating air space in between. Vertical and horizontal steel reinforcing rods were placed into grooves formed by pairs of blocks, and then a grout of cement and sand was poured inside. Warp and woof were woven together like a fabric of sturdy concrete.

Wright expected his clients to cast their own one-by-two-foot blocks. Most threw up their hands at the complicated task, but not the Tracys. After their drawings were completed in 1955, they worked for a year making and finishing 1,700 blocks in eleven configurations for their 1,200-square-foot home. With Stricker supervising, the builder Ray Brandes—himself the owner of a Wright house in nearby Issaquah—was able to get the house up in four months for a cost of $25,000, finishing in late 1956. Even though Wright declared in 1928 that concrete

The dining alcove (opposite, top left and right) has an easy relationship with the terrace outside. William Tracy followed Wright's design to build the redwood dining set. The living area's banquette (bottom) is also upholstered in a golden nylon the owners chose to represent sunlight. In its stair-stepped niche, the fireplace opens to both the dining and living areas. The concrete blocks paint ever-changing pictures on the walls and floor. Inset with glass, the back terrace wall (above) disappears into a lacy fabric.

Paired with the low coffered ceiling made of concrete blocks, redwood paneling warms up the bedrooms. Light emanates subtly from the built-in bookcases. "With the building closed in," recall the Tracys, "it soon became apparent that something new was coming to life here.... The perforated block patterns cast upon the vibrant, earth-colored floor, the pervasive scent of redwood, the textured walls and ceilings, all must have contributed to it."

"has neither song nor story," they named it Arietta—a short aria with a large voice.

"One of the remarkable things about this design was what genius was able to make out of such a small lot," observes William of the Tracys' property, less than an acre in size. "It's pretty much a city lot, but you don't sense that ... at all." Wright increased the house's footprint by reaching out with steps and a garden wall in front and a terrace in back framing their cliffside view of the water. Three bedrooms are placed in line with the entry on the private side, separated from the kitchen and utility core by a narrow hall. The L-shaped living area on the other side curls around a fireplace carved out of concrete blocks and stepped down to focus all eyes on it. Tucked around the corner is a spacious dining alcove. Supporting columns are inset with glass to make them almost transparent, as are the corners. When the French doors are open to the terrace beyond, any dividing line between indoors and out becomes immaterial.

Wright aggrandized space in the house, which was built on a square two-by-two-foot grid that unifies the house horizontally as the blocks do vertically. From the low six-foot-six-inch ceilings in the bedrooms, heights rise another two feet over the living area and then gain three more feet to make the kitchen and bathroom burst their small confines. Solid blocks melt away into natural windows where glass is substituted. Built-ins open up floor space. Heating is out of sight, embedded in the concrete floor. "We are of the opinion that this house is a work of art and that works of art are by nature mysteries. It has been a transcendental experience," say the Tracys, who have never left.

FEATURES

- The owners' construction help saved on labor costs.
- Eleven types of concrete block, cast by hand, form the walls inside and out.
- Set at an angle on its lot, the house nestles into the contours of the land to capture a wide view.
- A cascade of entry steps and a garden wall tying the carport to the house increase the footprint.
- The public side, shielding the bedrooms, is relatively closed, while the private side is open.
- The terrace fronting the living and dining areas serves as an outdoor room.

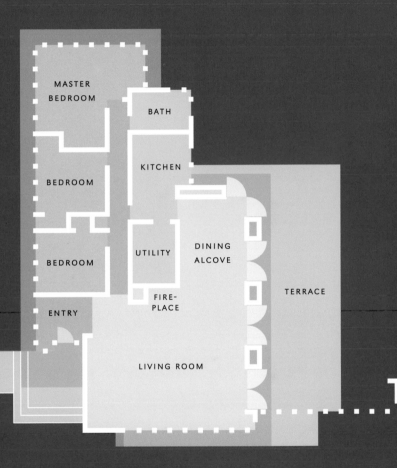

- Greater height emphasizes the living areas over the bedrooms, which are cavelike in contrast to the openness of the rest of the house.
- The four-inch concrete pad holds heating coils set into gravel.
- To reduce expenses the owners substituted redwood for steel specified for the French doors.
- A two-foot-square grid unifies all spaces.

CARPORT

MASTER BEDROOM

BEDROOM

BEDROOM

ENTRY

BATH

KITCHEN

UTILITY

FIRE-PLACE

DINING ALCOVE

LIVING ROOM

TERRACE

N

.085 INCH = 1 FOOT

If Wright's larger houses are architectural biographies, then cottages such as this must be seen as mystical haiku. Its lines are few and serve to celebrate nature. At 880 square feet, the lakeside cabin in south-central Wisconsin that Seth Peterson persuaded the ninety-one-year-old architect to design for him in 1958 is little more than gossamer shelter under a soaring roof. It may be one of the smallest of Wright's small commissions, but its story is probably the most poignant.

Peterson became a Wright devotée while still in high school and made it his life's ambition to join the Taliesin Fellowship, the architect's school. Having neither the needed experience nor the tuition, he was turned down and drifted into employment as a computer programmer for the state after serving in the army. But Peterson, then twenty-two, continued to tilt at his own personal windmill—the sage of Taliesin—up on the hilltop not far from his own home. Once Peterson offered the master an advance on his fee, Wright and his apprentice John Howe got to work.

Never one to forget unbuilt designs of his, the architect pulled a 1947 summer cottage plan out of his sleeve and adapted it using other recent work. For Peterson's site on a bluff overlooking Mirror Lake, the wizard of small spaces produced a one-room house focused entirely on the view. The materials were limited to three: sandstone quarried nearby, Philippine mahogany, and glass. The raked roof, even more than the roughly laid stone, is the lookout's signature. A shed roof was chosen for the main living area probably because, as Wright noted in 1954, "you get more for your money than you can get

IMPOSSIBLE DREAM

The Peterson Cottage

Furniture designed by Wright but never built was finally made during the restoration, together with related new chairs created by John Eifler for the living and dining areas (opposite). At the same time gravity heating coils were installed beneath the flagstone floor, as originally intended. Stylized pines in the wood cutouts of the clerestory windows are the cottage's only obvious ornament (above). Wright designed a similar lakeside cottage in Minnesota for Virginia and Donald Lovness that they did not build until 1972.

To the architecture critic Paul Goldberger, the experience of moving from the Peterson Cottage's cavelike bedroom out into the tall glassed-in living area is the "architectural expression of wakening, a . . . return to the world." After a visit he noted, "It was not merely for economy that he designed the bedroom to be as small, and as enclosed, as it is; it is nothing but a protective tent, symbolizing the night as the great space symbolizes the day." Clerestory windows reduce the amount of morning light that filters into the bedroom. The built-in bench also converts to a bed.

from another form of roof." Two flat roofs, low over the bedroom and high over the kitchen, belie the cottage's description as a "building all under one roof."

A flagstone entry terrace flows effortlessly into the flagstone floor inside and then out onto a generous side terrace. At the heart of the house rises a rusticated sandstone hearth, around which all space flows. Other than at the bathroom and the pantry, no internal doors interfere with movement. The ceiling, kept to six feet, eight inches over the cocoonlike bedroom, explodes to twelve feet at the edge of the living area. This roofline instantly makes the small cottage feel larger, an effect enhanced by window walls framed only in narrow wooden supports.

Construction had not even gotten under way before Wright died, on April 9, 1959. Peterson continued on, doing some of the work himself to save money and readying the home for his fiancée. But costs kept escalating despite cutbacks, and for uncertain reasons the young man who loved Wright's work took his own life the next year, as the cottage neared completion.

It was eventually acquired as part of Mirror Lake State Park but sat abandoned for decades until a band of concerned neighbors formed the Seth Peterson Cottage Conservancy, raised funds, and retained John Eifler to lead the $350,000 restoration. Peterson's dream is now shared with pretend Wright clients: the cottage that has "more architecture per square foot than any building Wright ever built," according to Wright's associate William Wesley Peters, is one of the few Wright houses to accept overnight guests.

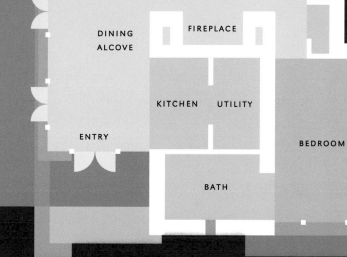

TERRACE

LIVING ROOM

DINING
ALCOVE

FIREPLACE

KITCHEN UTILITY

ENTRY

BEDROOM

BATH

FEATURES

- A living room, dining alcove, kitchen, bed-room, bathroom, and storage are all packed into 880 square feet.
- The upward-tilting shed roof gives what Wright called a "sense of overhead uplift," increasing the feeling of spaciousness.
- Glass walls on three sides create an openness to nature.
- Mitered corner windows eliminate obstruc-tions to the view.
- The southwestern exposure ushers in winter light, while the roof's broad overhang pro-vides summer shade.
- The cottage's stone, wood, and glass blend easily into the wooded lakeside setting.

> "With the massive appearance of the block construction, and the house rising out of the mountainside as it does, the home has a look of grandeur, even though it is designed and built to intimate scale."

John Rattenbury, *Phoenix Home/Garden,* January 1984

DESERT ROSE

The Lykes House

As if carved from the desert floor, the house grows organically from its landscape (opposite, top left and right). The tall drum next to the chimney holds an office above the kitchen. A clerestory rings the living area. In the walled garden, the pool's half-moon shape echoes the windows that look out onto it from the kitchen and the office above (bottom left and right). Portholes screen the view out over the Valley of the Sun, maintaining Wright's circular theme.

For Wright circles symbolized infinity, a world without end. He became fascinated with them early in his career, hanging balloons in the barrel-vaulted playroom in Oak Park he built for his children in 1895 and immortalizing them among flags in an art glass parade for the Coonley Playhouse (1912). Circles also starred in a colorful mural for Chicago's Midway Gardens (1913) and bubbled onto cabaret china (1922) at the Imperial Hotel in Tokyo. But not until about 1938 did Wright bring these circular forms to earth as the basis for a house plan. His proposal for the Jester House that year called for circular pavilions tied together by a patio, inviting a daily agenda of indoor-outdoor living. More circles figured in later Wright designs, from the solar hemicycle built as the second Jacobs House (1944) and a house of circles created for his son David Wright in 1950 to the world-famous Guggenheim Museum (1956) in New York City.

In 1959 circles flowed from his pen once again, for the last of the four hundred houses he designed during his seventy-year career. In May 1958, when Wright was almost ninety-one, Norman Lykes beseeched the architect to design a house in Phoenix for himself, his wife, Aimee, and their three children. A shipping magnate, he included a request for a workshop in which to pursue his inventions and specified a cost: "in the neighborhood of $55,000"—certainly more than many of Wright's clients were budgeting. Wright must have liked the sum, for he agreed.

The Lykes family came to Wright through John Rattenbury, one of the architect's associates at Taliesin who had designed a number of small items for them. When Rattenbury showed Wright photographs of some of the sites the client was considering, he

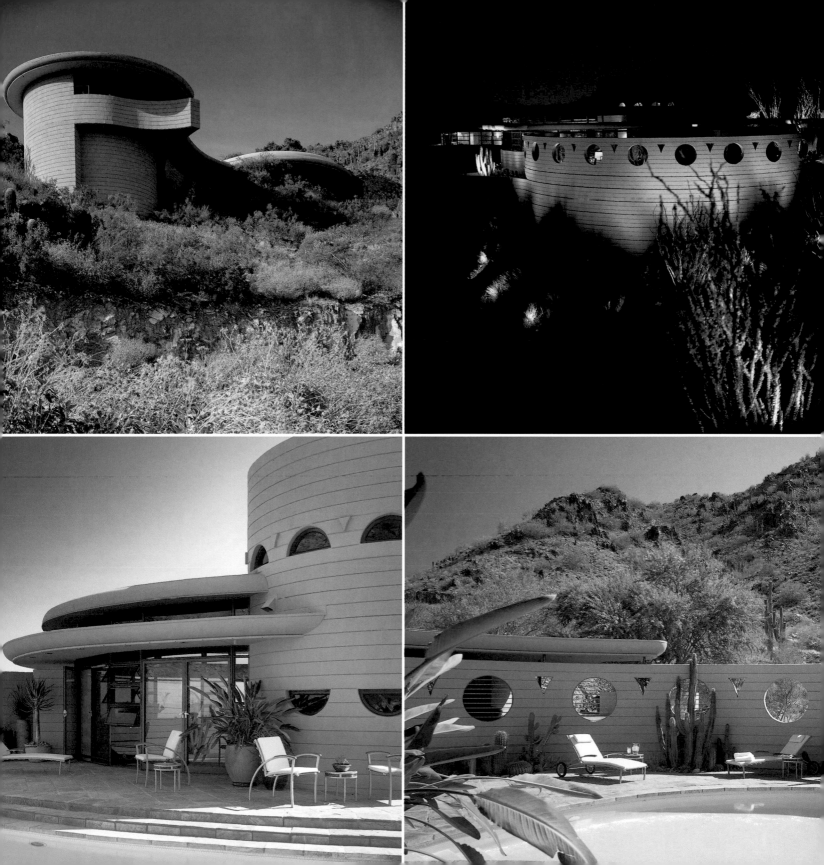

dismissed them. "These are very uninteresting lots. Encourage them to find something better." After being advised that "Mr. Wright wanted more of a challenge," Lykes found an acre of steeply sloping land in Saguaro Canyon with panoramic views of Phoenix below. "Tell them to buy it," instructed Wright. In March 1959 Rattenbury gave the architect a topographic map of the property. "He set it aside and worked on something else," Rattenbury later recalled. "The next morning he asked for the topo map and at once started to sketch out a plan right on the sheet.... There was a beautiful rock formation at the edge which he wanted to save."

Wright first drew two embracing circles, a living room with a view of the valley and a garden court walled in for privacy. The spheres collided like the circles on the playful Imperial Hotel china. "They can look upwards, over the court wall, and see the surrounding mountains," Rattenbury remembered Wright saying. "The bedrooms will wrap around the hillside, on the far side of the house. Every room will have a view. We will save the rock outcropping." The next week Wright died on April 9.

Rattenbury finished the presentation drawings, but although the Lykeses loved the house they postponed construction until 1963 and it was not finished until 1968, at a cost of $140,000. Rattenbury added a workshop off the entry and a circular office elevated above the circular kitchen, all to be shaped with concrete blocks. Care was taken to protect the site, with footings dug by hand instead of backhoe and the blocks hand carried up the hill by schoolboys instead of trucks.

Tinted a soft rose to blend into its desert home, the house

In the living area (opposite) Wright's "origami" chairs hold a conversation before the fire. The dining table beyond is ringed with copies of his barrel chairs, a famous circular design from his Prairie years. The concrete blocks and the window muntins follow the same grid pattern (top). Recalling the Guggenheim Museum, circles cascade down the ziggurat-shaped fireplace to reinforce the house's motif (above). Steps at left lead up to the office.

Like a celestial orb, a skylight floods the upper-level office with sunlight (above). Semicircular lunettes provide not only light but also integral ornament for the room, a theme echoed by the Fortuny lamp. The contrasting metal chairs are by Warren McArthur. More curves overtake the kitchen below (right), which has been updated with a new stainless-steel counter and cabinets to match the originals. Stools and a movable table don't miss a beat. Pairing the windows upstairs and down would produce perfect circles.

clearly meets Wright's dictum of being of the hill, not on it. Its 2,500 square feet swirl around the rocky hillside, naturally embracing the site in a way no hard edges could. A large drum holding the living area is balanced at the opposite end by a cozier cylinder secluding the master suite. A gallery arcs in between, leading originally to five bedrooms open to the mountain-ringed vista below. The in-line plan, like so many Wright designed, adroitly zones the house into living areas and quieter sleeping rooms. Beyond the dining nook and the kitchen, a terrace balloons into a walled garden, now home to a pool.

Small circles flow into larger circles, one sphere bisects another, arcs scribe an uncompleted radius. Semicircular portholes serve as eyes for the walls, inspecting the view. Round skylights shower the house with circles of light. More portholes interspersed with triangles dot exterior walls, integrating Wright's module into the house's fabric. Mirroring the human body itself, the rounded shapes are humanizing. Circles reach out like arms to enclose rooms with a comforting hug, heightening their sense of intimacy by removing all the corners.

Wright chose concrete block, raked between the units to emphasize the horizontal line, because it easily accommodated the design's circular forms. In his last years he had rescued concrete from "the gutter" and shown how in the right hands it could be as malleable as plastic and as artistic as stone. "Herein the despised thing becomes at least a thoroughbred and a sound *mechanical* means to a rare and beautiful use as an architect's medium, as the 'block' becomes a mere mechanical unit in a quiet, plastic whole," he suggested

A terrace expands the enlarged master bedroom (opposite, top left). Next door, a guest room (top right) was created from two original bedrooms. Mahogany woodwork in the dressing area and paneling behind the bed in the master suite (bottom left and right) make the sleeping areas feel restful. Glistening glass and copper tilework used in the master suite's shower (above) pick up earthy tones used throughout the house for the renovation.

Wright liked to turn every space, even hallways, to practical uses. Built-in bookcases line the entrance hall as well as the gallery leading to the bedrooms. In the entry, which steps up to give the gallery more prominence, 1950s pottery fills the mahogany shelves.

in 1928. Inexpensive, impressionable, easy to color—concrete is humble only before "imagination enters," he modestly noted.

When a new owner purchased the house in 1993, it was structurally sound but in need of a facelift inside. She updated the interior in a way that respected the Wrightian vision but was comfortably stylish. Mahogany paneling that warms up the concrete walls was refinished, copper screens were added, metal trim was coated with a matching coppery enamel, and orange exterior paint was removed, returning the walls to a dusty rose that blends in beside the desert cactus. The concrete floor, by then cracked, was replaced with a coppery slate. New furnishings and fabrics reflecting the owner's fondness for rich colors joined the built-ins and original pieces designed for the house. Four bedrooms in the "polliwog tail"—sized originally to fit small children—were revamped, resulting in a larger master bedroom, a generous guest room, and a den. Two original bathrooms remain in between, while a luxurious master bath was carved out of the original space in the toe of the house. Norman Lykes's workshop was converted into a media room. And now visible from the kitchen's semicircular windows is a pool whose aquamarine waters etch the same shape into the floor of the walled garden.

With its new lease on life, the house has come full circle—a compact house reinterpreted for a new century. "The home rests on the desert mountain terrain like some gentle bird momentarily poised on a rock outcropping," observes Bruce Brooks Pfeiffer in *Frank Lloyd Wright Monograph, 1951-1959* (1988). "Were the house to 'fly away,' the desert would still be there, as it has since time began, untouched."

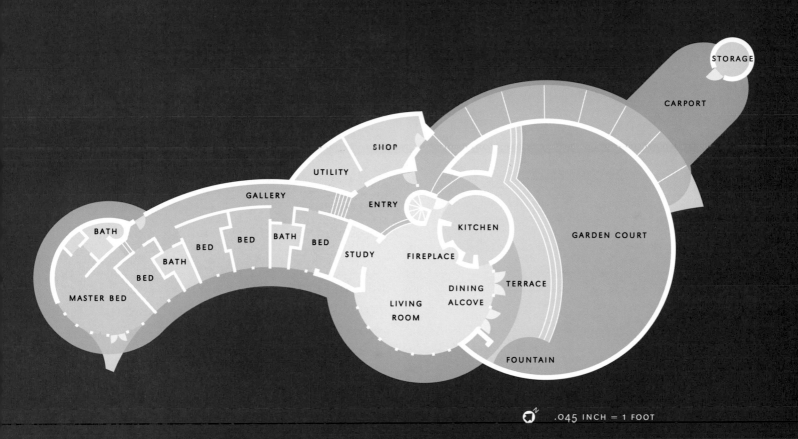

STORAGE

CARPORT

SHOP

UTILITY

GALLERY

ENTRY

BATH

KITCHEN

GARDEN COURT

BED

BED

BATH

BED

STUDY

FIREPLACE

BATH

BED

TERRACE

DINING
ALCOVE

MASTER BED

LIVING
ROOM

FOUNTAIN

.045 INCH = 1 FOOT

F E A T U R E S

- The circular plan reflects the shape of the site's natural plateau and fits into the mountainside without disturbing the land.
- A desert rose tint blends the concrete blocks into the landscape.
- Wide roof brims provide shade and capture breezes.
- Panoramic windows topped by a clerestory frame distant vistas from the private side while semicircular portholes discreetly limit views from the street.
- Circular skylights channel light into the house from above.

- The terrace and garden court, with its new pool (added to the original plan above), create an outdoor room larger than the living area.
- Circular spaces eliminate corners, making rooms more naturally inviting.
- Changing ceiling and floor levels add variety yet maintain human scale.
- Spaces flow into one another, held together by intersecting circles and segments.
- The entrance hall and bedroom corridor do double duty as storage and display space.
- The bedrooms proved flexible enough to allow for enlargement through recombination.

> "Smaller spaces create intimacy and synergies between people, as well as opportunity to exercise patience and compassion and community. You can't run away from friction or unresolved conflict."

Susan Jacobs Lockhart, 2003

ALL ABOUT LIGHT

The Lockhart Cottage

"The desert has become my spiritual home," says Susan Jacobs Lockhart of her cottage (opposite, top), "and this is a place of refuge and prospect within that larger home. Its spaces are in scale with the desert foliage, not imposing themselves. There is a dialogue of equality and therefore respect." Terraces help the house spread out into the desert, where its native boulders subtly blend in. The same rustic desert masonry was used for the fireplace (bottom left), a holdover from an old cabana. Lockhart uses an alcove of the house's living room (bottom right) to work on her art glass commissions. "In spite of the turn of fashion," she says, "I have not chosen to change the furnishings. The moss greens and yellows are wonderful colors compatible with the desert—like sunshine."

Susan Jacobs Lockhart has never been fazed by living in a 450-square-foot cottage or by the 150-square-foot desert cabana that preceded it. Her parents, Katherine and Herbert Jacobs, commissioned not one but two Wright houses themselves (including the first one profiled on pages 102–7). She grew up in those compact Wright homes, has spent nearly a half century associated with Wright's Taliesin Fellowship, and with one of the architect's early apprentices built a home in the desert just an eight-minute walk from Wright's Taliesin West in Scottsdale, Arizona.

"The fact that we did not have a lot of money kept life simpler," she recently recalled. "The consumer generation was not mine or my parents'. Our values centered on the quality of life, the art of enjoying small things, the richness of friends and intellectual stimulation, of books, of nature, of healthy food prepared simply, with interesting friends to share it. I came to regard light as an essential ingredient of life, with full-length glass to view sun and moon, changes in season, birds and wildlife and desert growth close at hand."

Lockhart's desert shelter was designed not by Wright but by her late husband, Kenneth Lockhart, a longtime Taliesin architect who supervised projects from the late 1930s until the early 1990s. Yet her tiny home shares the attributes of the small residences that Wright spent his life perfecting. It is no bigger than it needed to be for two persons, it takes its materials and colors from the surrounding landscape, it contains mysteries even within its small footprint, it requires little maintenance beyond painting of the fascia boards, its built-ins conserve space, its terraces create outdoor rooms, its glass doors frame ever-changing pictures of nature.

"I love the scale of the rooms, the levels of intimacy and comfort," says Lockhart, an artist known for her glass designs in the Wrightian spirit. "I live in the whole space every moment I am there."

When the Lockharts were married in 1964, they decided to forego the "urban" environment of the apprentices' quarters at Taliesin West, opting instead for the desert "countryside." Susan, who came to Taliesin in 1958, had already lived in a nine-by-nine-foot tent. The couple moved into one of the experimental desert shelters traditionally built by Wright's apprentices, this one last occupied by John Howe, the architect's principal draftsman. Made of canvas, wood, and low masonry walls with a fireplace but no bathroom, the cabana was a snug fit for a few years.

In 1968 they began to plan a somewhat larger house on the same site, complete with modern necessities and ceilings high enough for the six-foot, one-inch Kenn. Their goal was to keep a low profile on the rise of land, oriented with views to the south and protected on the west. Building on land owned by the Frank Lloyd Wright Foundation, they chose to use the desert masonry materials and design grammar of Taliesin West. "The house was designed to embrace nature totally," says Lockhart, "visually and by walking out into it with no break between terrace and desert." The couple also based their unit system on the thirty- and sixty-degree angles established by the fireplace they inherited.

It took them the better part of a decade to finish, building the house stone by stone. Susan gathered rubble and the boulders that, like Taliesin West, form the distinctive masonry; she also mixed the concrete in which they are set. Kenn built trenches for the utilities, did the framing and carpentry, and molded the

"We joke about the kitchen being a "one-and-a-half-butt space," says Lockhart. "Two adults do a do-si-do, but Kenn and I both cooked here together for parties up to twelve people" (opposite, top left). Built-in shelves hold her stemware (top right). In the bedroom (bottom left and right), a built-in desk and bookshelves organize Lockhart's carefully culled personal belongings. Glass doors to the left of the bed lead outside onto a second terrace. Using the terrace (below), she can accommodate up to forty guests.

Having to put Susan's plywood work table in the middle of the living room soon impelled the couple to begin a separate studio (top). Although started in the late 1980s, the 350-square-foot space she designed was not completed until 1998, with the help of Joe Fabris. With its hideaway bed, kitchenette, bathroom, and walk-in closet, it doubles as a studio and a guesthouse. Her table and storage cabinets, both on wheels, move easily. Here she creates sandblasted glass sculptures (above) and designs other commissions in stained glass to be made off site. "The house and studio are all about light," observes Lockhart. "Light is all-important for me in my creative world as in my residential world."

walls. Susan upholstered the furnishings and appliquéd the draperies with one of her own designs. First they built the bedroom, bathroom, and east terrace—living in the old cabana and then moving into the bedroom while they constructed the living room, study, and kitchen. After three years of this "casserole living," remembers Lockhart, "I stood in the doorway and looked at the new rooms and thought, How can I possibly live in all that space? It seemed so large, almost intimidating."

No right angles, except in the bathroom, exist to confine space. "The triangulation of the thirty- and sixty-degree walls keeps the eye discovering around the next corner, as if you could hide in such a small space!" she notes. "When you sit down, the six-foot, seven-inch ceiling height creates a very intimate space that also invites you to visually travel through the south-facing windows onto the terrace, which acts as an extension of the living room."

Lockhart has found small spaces "transformational." As she explains, "They make you conscious of what things you surround yourself with and keep you from mindlessly saving everything. We were not collectors of 'stuff' except books. I have spent most of my life," she adds, "in compact, comforting, and visually nurturing spaces. They offer an opportunity to show respect for sharing and respect for another's need for separateness. In many large houses, each person has a separate zone and there is no need to exercise any of these aspects of what it is to be human." Now she calls the desert rabbits, quail, owls, coyotes, bobcats, mice, rocks, plants, and trees her friends. If ever she leaves, she hopes that the Foundation will give her visiting privileges.

FEATURES

Although not designed by Wright, the house embodies his principles right on his doorstep.

- At a compact 450 square feet, the cottage has accommodated two persons with relative ease.
- The Lockharts contributed all the labor, including plumbing and electrical work, keeping costs to a minimum.
- Walls of desert masonry outside and inside blend into the landscape and repeat the materials used for Taliesin West nearby.
- Thirty- and sixty-degree angles eliminate hard corners, gently guiding the eye around spaces.
- The kitchen acts like an alcove of the living room, balanced at the other end by an alcove holding Lockhart's drawing board.
- The scored concrete floor extends onto terraces, expanding the living space almost year-round in this warm climate.
- Accordion doors conserve space in the kitchen, bedroom, and bathroom.
- Hexagonal tables fit together like a honeycomb for dining by the twelve-foot-long built-in sofa in the living room.
- A 350-square-foot studio-guesthouse has given Lockhart extra space for her work.

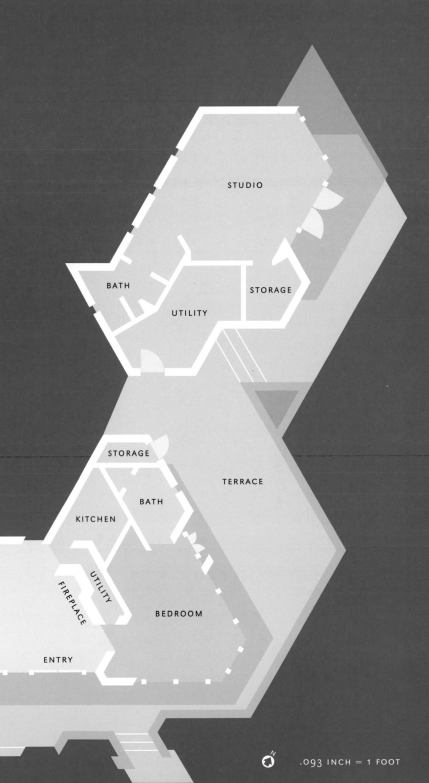

.093 INCH = 1 FOOT

VISITING WRIGHT'S SMALL HOUSES

The following small houses by Frank Lloyd Wright are open regularly or occasionally for visitation; several may be closed temporarily for restoration. Please call ahead to confirm availability, tour hours, and admission fees.

Affleck House
c/o College of Architecture
Lawrence Technological University
1925 North Woodward Avenue
Bloomfield Hills, MI 48013
248-204-2880

Barton House
118 Summit Avenue
Buffalo, NY 14214
716-856-3858
www.darwinmartinhouse.org
info@darwinmartinhouse.org

Cheney House
Bed and Breakfast
520 North East Avenue
Oak Park, IL 60302
708-524-2067
http://oakparknet.com

Frank Lloyd Wright Home and Studio
951 Chicago Avenue
Oak Park, IL 60302
708-848-1978
www.wrightplus.org

Freeman House
c/o University of Southern California
School of Architecture
1962 Glencoe Way
Los Angeles, CA 90068
213-740-2723
www.usc.edu/dept/architecture/slide/
Freeman

Gordon House
The Oregon Garden
879 West Main Street
Silverton, OR 97381
503-874-6006
877-674-2733, ext. 6006
www.oregongarden.org

Kentuck Knob
P.O. Box 305
Chalk Hill, PA 15421
724-329-1901
www.kentuck-knob.com

May House
450 Madison Avenue, Southeast
Grand Rapids, MI 49503
616-246-4821

Peterson Cottage
E9982 Fern Dell Road
Lake Delton, WI 53940
608-254-6051 (tours)
608-254-6551 (rentals)
www.sethpeterson.org

Pope-Leighey House
at Woodlawn Plantation
9000 Richmond Highway
Alexandria, VA 22309
703-780-4000
www.nationaltrust.org

Rosenbaum House
601 Riverview Drive
Florence, AL 35630
256-740-8899
www.florenceal.org
bbroach@florenceal.org

Stockman House
530 First Street, N.E.
Mason City, IA 50401
641-423-1923/421-3666

Zimmerman House
c/o Currier Gallery of Art
201 Myrtle Way
Manchester, NH 03104
603-669-6144, ext. 102
www.currier.org

SELECTED BIBLIOGRAPHY

BOOKS

Aguar, Charles E. and Berdeana. *Wright-scapes: Frank Lloyd Wright's Landscape Designs.* New York: McGraw-Hill, 2002.

Blake, Peter. *The Master Builders: Le Corbusier, Mies van der Rohe, Frank Lloyd Wright.* New York: Norton, 1976.

Dunham, Judith. *Details of Frank Lloyd Wright: The California Work, 1909–1974.* San Francisco: Chronicle, 1994.

Eifler, John, and Kristin Visser. *Frank Lloyd Wright's Seth Peterson Cottage: Rescuing a Lost Masterwork.* 1997. 2d ed. Madison, Wis.: Prairie Oak Press, 1999.

Futagawa, Yukio, and Bruce Brooks Pfeiffer. *Frank Lloyd Wright Monographs.* Vols. 3 and 8. Tokyo: ADA Edita, 1988.

Gebhard, David. *Romanza: The California Architecture of Frank Lloyd Wright.* San Francisco: Chronicle, 1988.

Gill, Brendan. *Many Masks: A Life of Frank Lloyd Wright.* New York: Putnam, 1987.

Hanks, David. *The Decorative Designs of Frank Lloyd Wright.* 1979. Reprint, New York: Dover, 1999.

Hitchcock, Henry-Russell. *In the Nature of Materials: The Buildings of Frank Lloyd Wright, 1887–1941.* 1942. Reprint, New York: Da Capo, 1969.

Hoffmann, Donald. *Frank Lloyd Wright: Architecture and Nature.* New York: Dover, 1986.

———. *Understanding Frank Lloyd Wright's Architecture.* New York: Dover, 1995.

Kalec, Don. "The Jacobs House I," in *Frank Lloyd Wright and Madison: Eight Decades of Artistic and Social Interaction.* Madison, Wis.: Elvehjem Museum of Art, University of Wisconsin, 1990.

Legler, Dixie. *Frank Lloyd Wright: The Western Work.* San Francisco: Chronicle, 1999.

———. *Prairie Style: Houses and Gardens by Frank Lloyd Wright and the Prairie School.* New York: Stewart, Tabori and Chang, 1999.

Lind, Carla. *Frank Lloyd Wright's Glass Designs.* Wright at a Glance Series. San Francisco: Pomegranate, 1995.

———. *The Wright Style.* New York: Simon and Schuster, 1992.

McCarter, Robert, ed. *Frank Lloyd Wright: A Primer on Architectural Principles.* New York: Princeton Architectural Press, 1991.

Morton, Terry B., ed. *The Pope-Leighey House.* Washington, D.C.: National Trust for Historic Preservation, 1969.

Pfeiffer, Bruce Brooks. *Frank Lloyd Wright: The Masterworks.* New York: Rizzoli, 1993.

Reisley, Roland, with John Timpane. *Usonia, New York: Building a Community with Frank Lloyd Wright.* New York: Princeton Architectural Press, 2001.

Rosenbaum, Alvin. *Usonia: Frank Lloyd Wright's Design for America.* Washington, D.C.: Preservation Press, 1993.

Sanderson, Arlene, ed. *Wright Sites: A Guide to Frank Lloyd Wright Public Places.* New York: Princeton Architectural Press, 1995.

Secrest, Meryle. *Frank Lloyd Wright.* New York: Knopf, 1992.

Sergeant, John. *Frank Lloyd Wright's Usonian Houses: The Case for Organic Architecture.* New York: Whitney Library of Design, 1976.

Storrer, William Allin. *The Frank Lloyd Wright Companion.* Chicago: University of Chicago Press, 1993.

Visser, Kristin. *Frank Lloyd Wright and the Prairie School in Wisconsin.* Madison, Wis.: Prairie Oak Press, 1992.

Wright, Frank Lloyd. *Frank Lloyd Wright: Collected Writings.* 5 vols. Edited by Bruce Brooks Pfeiffer. New York: Rizzoli, 1992–95.

PERIODICALS AND REPORTS

"America's Housing, 1900–2010," in *Housing Facts, Figures and Trends.* Washington, D.C.: National Association of Home Builders, 2001.

Bernstein, Fred A. "Renovating Frank Lloyd (W)right." *Metropolitan Home,* November-December 1997.

Besner, Guy. "Modern Architecture in Seattle: Tracy Usonian Automatic House." 2000. Unpublished.

De Reus, Jim. "What We Learned from Frank Lloyd Wright." *House and Home,* February 1959.

Denson, Lynda Horton. "Harmony and Serenity: Wright House Preserves a Master's Poetry." *Chicago Tribune,* August 21, 1998.

Eifler, John. "Restoring the Jacobs House." *Fine Homebuilding,* April–May 1993.

"FLLW's Characteristic Double-Decker Flat Top." *House and Home,* April 1955.

"Frank Lloyd Wright: His Contribution to the Beauty of American Life." *House Beautiful,* November 1955.

"Frank Lloyd Wright and the Natural House." *House and Home,* January 1955.

Goldberger, Paul. "Where Earth and Sky Meet: A Wright Cottage, for Rent." *New York Times,* June 2, 1994.

Gordon, Elizabeth. "Exploding the Box to Gain Spaciousness." *House Beautiful,* October 1959.

Hill, John deKoven. "Interior Space as Architectural Poetry." *House Beautiful,* October 1959.

"How Big Can a Tiny House Be?" *House and Home,* March 1954.

Jacobs, Herbert. "Our Wright Houses." *Historic Preservation,* July–September 1976.

Kullman, Joe. "The Wright Stuff." *Phoenix Home/Garden,* January 1984.

Lockhart, Susan Jacobs. "Architecture as Transformational Space" and "Art as Light and Light as Art." *Frank Lloyd Wright Quarterly,* spring 2003.

McCoy, Jerry A. "The Stockman House." *Frank Lloyd Wright Quarterly,* summer 1991.

McCoy, Robert E. "Rock Crest–Rock Glen: Prairie School Planning in Iowa." *Prairie School Review,* third quarter, 1968.

————. "The Stockman House: A Cameo of Wright's Prairie School Design." 2002. Unpublished.

Mosher, Robert. "The Eloquence of Materials." *House Beautiful,* November 1955.

Rattenbury, John. "The Lykes House." n.d. Unpublished.

"Seven Lessons from Frank Lloyd Wright." *House and Home,* November 1954.

Sturges, George and Selma. Interview with Indira Berndtson, Frank Lloyd Wright Foundation, March 29, 1992.

Sullivan, Ann C. "Preservation Technology: Re-Creating Wright." *Architecture,* August 1997.

"Thirty-two Simple and Basic Design Ideas of Frank Lloyd Wright." *House and Home,* September 1956.

"This New House by Frank Lloyd Wright Is a Rich Textbook of the Principles He Pioneered." *House and Home,* March 1953.

Tilton + Lewis Associates, Chicago. *Historic Structure Report for the Isadore J. and Lucille Zimmerman House.* October 1989.

Tracy, William and Martha. "A Work of Art." ca. 1990. Unpublished.

"Wright Interlocks Site and Structure." *House Beautiful,* October 1959.

"The Wrightian Look Built into an Existing Structure." *House Beautiful,* October 1959.

"Your Heritage from Frank Lloyd Wright." *House Beautiful,* October 1959.

PHOTOGRAPH CREDITS

Ping Amranand: 110, 114 (top)

Gordon Beall: 47

Judith Bromley: 44, 45 (all)

Currier Gallery of Art: 120 (both), 121, 123

Michael Freeman: 4 (top and bottom left), 6–7, 42 (both), 48–49, 63 (bottom left), 68, 117–18

Pedro E. Guerrero: 1, 8, 14 (all), 17 (both), 18 (top and bottom left), 19 (both), 149–52

Tom Heinz: 12, 13, 18 (bottom right)

Biff Henrich, Keystone Productions: 37

Carol M. Highsmith: 30, 75

Balthazar Korab: 16 (bottom), 24–25, 28–29, 33, 34–35, 36, 52–53, 63 (bottom right), 73, 79, 109, 139 (top left)

Christian Korab: 4 (top right), 10, 20–21, 59, 88–92, 94–100

Andrew Lautman: 69

James C. Massey: 16 (top)

Norman McGrath: 50, 51

Jon Miller, Hedrich Blessing: 9, 61, 76 (top left)

National Trust for Historic Preservation (Ron Blunt): 108, 111, 112, 113, 114 (bottom)

River City Society for Historic Preservation: 11 (both)

Paul Rocheleau: 15, 31, 38, 60, 64, 65, 71, 72, 76 (top right, bottom left and right), 80, 85, 102–7, 122, 124–26

Rosenbaum House: 46

Seth Peterson Cottage Conservancy: 134 (Pella, Inc.), 135 (Mark Vlaidik), 136 (Eric Wallner)

Judy A. Slagle: 26

Steelcase Inc.: 54, 55, 63 (top left and right), 82, 84

Tim Street-Porter: 2, 3, 4 (bottom right), 39, 82–83, 86–87, 139 (top right, bottom left and right), 140–46

Alexander Vertikoff: 27

Scot Zimmerman: 22, 23, 40, 40–41, 43, 57, 58, 67, 70, 74, 129–32

Endpapers and plans by Robert L. Wiser

Original Lockhart Cottage plan courtesy Susan Jacobs Lockhart

ACKNOWLEDGMENTS

I am especially indebted to Dixie Legler, a fellow author on Frank Lloyd Wright, for her assistance in compiling research on the topics presented in this book. Her knowledge of Wright, good humor, and continuing friendship have been invaluable. Pedro E. Guerrero, who embarked on his photographic career with Wright's blessing in 1939 and returned to document Susan Jacobs Lockhart's desert cottage, remains an equally steadfast collaborator. To Lockhart and the many owners who have shared their Wright homes over the years also goes heartfelt appreciation. Special thanks are due Gail Kohl for her assistance, Robert Maddex for his help, Constance Herndon for her early support, and Richard Olsen and Eric Himmel at Harry N. Abrams for seeing the book to publication. Final kudos go to Robert Wiser, who always has the Wright stuff.

INDEX

Page references in italics indicate photographs.

Dedicated to Loren Pope, Mary Palmer, Roland and Ronny Reisley, Susan Jacobs Lockhart, and all the other owners of the small homes featured on these pages. In faithfully following the principles of Frank Lloyd Wright, they have paved a path for us all.

Commissioning Editor: Constance Herndon

Produced by Archetype Press, Inc.
Project Director: Diane Maddex
Research Assistants: Dixie Legler and Robert L. Maddex
Designer: Robert L. Wiser

Jacket: Isabel Roberts House (1908), River Forest, Illinois [Christian Korab]

Endpapers: Pope-Leighey House (1939), Alexandria, Virginia [Drawing by Robert L. Wiser]

Page 1: Frank Lloyd Wright inspecting Usonia Homes in Pleasantville, New York, 1949 [Pedro E. Guerrero]

Pages 2 and 3: La Miniatura (1923), Pasadena, California [Tim Street-Porter]

Pages 4 (top left) and 6–7: Sturges House (1939), Brentwood Heights, California [Michael Freeman]

Pages 4 (top right) and 20–21: Isabel Roberts House (1908), River Forest, Illinois [Christian Korab]

Pages 4 (bottom left) and 48–49: Jester-Pfeiffer House (1938/1971), Scottsdale, Arizona [Michael Freeman]

Pages 4 (bottom right) and 86–87: Lykes House (1959), Phoenix [Tim Street-Porter]

Library of Congress Cataloging-in-Publication Data

Maddex, Diane.

  Wright-sized houses : Frank Lloyd Wright's solutions for making small houses feel big / Diane Maddex

     p.   cm.

  Includes bibliographical references and index.

  ISBN 978-0-8109-4626-2

  1. Wright, Frank Lloyd, 1867–1959. 2. Small houses—United States. I. Title.

NA737.W7A4 2003a

728.37′092—dc21   2003006958

Published in 2003 by Abrams, an imprint of ABRAMS.

Printed and bound in Singapore

10   9   8   7   6

Abrams books are available at special discounts when purchased in quantity for premiums and promotions as well as fundraising or educational use. Special editions can also be created to specification. For details, contact specialsales@abramsbooks.com or the address below.

THE ART OF BOOKS SINCE 1949

115 West 18th Street
New York, NY 10011
www.abramsbooks.com